TEACHING LIBRARY USE COMPETENCE

LIBRARY ORIENTATION SERIES

TEACHING LIBRARY USE COMPETENCE:

BRIDGING THE GAP FROM HIGH SCHOOL TO COLLEGE

Papers Presented at the Eleventh Annual
Library Instruction Conference held at
Eastern Michigan University, May 7-8, 1981

edited by
Carolyn A. Kirkendall
Director, Project LOEX
Center of Educational Resources
Eastern Michigan University

Published for the
Center of Educational Resources,
Eastern Michigan University
by

Pierian Press
ANN ARBOR, MICHIGAN
1982

Library of Congress Catalog Card No. 82-62645
ISBN 0-87650-145-5

PIERIAN PRESS
P.O. Box 1808
Ann Arbor, Michigan 48106

Contents

Preface

Carolyn A. Kirkendall
Director
LOEX Clearinghouse

The Eleventh Annual Library Instruction Conference was held on May 7 & 8, 1981, at Eastern Michigan University. The meeting's name, after a decade of titled "Annual Conference on Library Orientation for Academic Libraries," was changed to reflect the more specialized topics currently under discussion in the bibliographic instruction field, and to include and recognize library instructors from all levels of education.

The printed presentations are included in the order they were presented, without stringent editing, to maintain the flavor and originality of each session: readers are again reminded that spoken presentations will always vary in readability.

Readers are also requested to bear in mind that each speaker was invited to contribute to the broad and general theme of the meeting, and while some of the speeches may appear to strain to address the issue at times, the connection was obvious to Conference participants. Indeed, attendees were reminded to compare presentations and to explore the applications of all sessions for timeliness and relevance.

This particular collection of speeches is the result of a suggestion received from a school media specialist who attended the Tenth Annual Orientation Conference. After sitting through the meetings, he shared three distinct impressions and conclusions:

---- his suspicions were confirmed concerning the ways that college librarians view the job that the schools are or are not doing to teach library use,

---- he was "very impressed with the commonality of concerns, problems, real and proposed solutions, and methods shared by the college people" and those in the schools, including "having to deal with exactly the same kinds of faculty and administrative resistance to the programs" that librarians are attempting to establish, and

---- he was left with the question, "Why aren't we talking to each other?"[1]

The Eleventh Annual Conference, *Teaching Library Use Competence: Bridging the Gap from High School to College*, was the attempt to establish this communication between teaching librarians from different school levels. It addressed related problems and issues reflected both in current literature and in past Conference presentations. For example, a decade before this meeting, speaker Millicent Palmer maintained:

> "This writer has heard university faculty say that if high school libraries did their job, library instruction wouldn't be necessary at the university level. Such comments indicate an abysmal ignorance of the differences between high school and university library resources and the knowledge required to use them. The idea of teaching high school students how to retrieve what they don't have is pedagogically untenable."[2]

And less than a month before this 1981 meeting, John Berry, in an editorial in *Library Journal*, mentions that he is heartened to see the sense of urgency with which academic librarians have organized to deal with the national crisis in library illiteracy, and he recommends the creation of a national-level body — cutting across type-of-library boundaries — devoted to developing a crash program of library instruction to reach all Americans.[3]

To further emphasize the relevance of the general Conference topic, Conference participants were reminded to read, in the same *Library Journal* issue, the remarks of the Director of Beloit College Library, who maintains that academic librarians are faced with the impossible task of trying to equip a great many students to deal with even the rudiments of library use, because the primary and secondary education of today's students is crippled by a lack of library knowledge. He states that most students enter higher education virtually without any inkling of how to use a library, so user education programs in academic libraries must be viewed as essentially remedial. Seen in this light, he continues, the problem of basic library orientation becomes properly the responsibility of the elementary and secondary school librarians since it is only they who can deal with it in other than a remedial sense. "Academic librarians must be relieved of the Sisyphean chore of dealing with the epidemic of library illiteracy now confronting them." And it is the school librarians, he concludes, who must see that students have knowledge of libraries and if they fail in this task, academic librarians will be forced to continue their largely ineffectual remedial efforts.[4]

Introduced through these attestations, the broad theme of the meeting, that of whether or not the entering college student is prepared to use libraries and what could be done to establish a link in the library instruction chain, was addressed by the Conference keynote speaker, who had conducted a local survey on library use preparation of incoming college freshmen students at her institution.

The state of library user education in United Kingdom schools was presented. A public librarian involved with library use instruction, who recognizes the need for a link in library skills knowledge among a diversity of patrons, shared his experiences. A media center testing specialist and two academic librarians shared their expertise on testing as a method for assessing library skills at three different educational levels. These presentations, with distributed test samples, were included on the agenda to provide practical advice to those confronted with the general problem of how to assess skills, and to illustrate what aids have been produced to solve this problem and to standardize assessment techniques.

Other speakers — media specialists — spoke specifically to the problems involved in establishing programs for secondary schools students in library skills. Two simulated library lessons were also scheduled, to vary the format and to illustrate how both academic and school librarians can effectively instruct in search strategy. The conflict between teaching librarians and classroom teachers was addressed. A program for entering freshmen who need instruction in how to conduct research was delineated by a university English professor.

These proceedings also include a copy of the guidelines suggested for group discussion, to illustrate that in these annual informal sessions, the connections and similarities of topics within the broad theme are addressed. Sample test instruments are also included, as well as a list of participants and an annotated bibliography of related articles published during 1980. The LOEX Director is grateful to librarians who coordinated these discussions.

The LOEX office is also thankful — as always — to the publishers who provide continuous support and generosity in sponsoring the annual parties at the Conference: Neal-Schuman Publishers, Inc. and Pierian Press. The efficient and helpful McKenny Union staff support is also appreciated, as is the excellent assistance provided by Paul Borawski of the University's Continuing Education Division. Special thanks go to Hannelore Rader who prepared the bibliography, and, most importantly, to the cast of enthusiastic speakers who shared their time, expertise and experience so capably.

NOTES

1. Letter from Ed Marman — Marshall Junior High School, Wayne, Michigan; May 12, 1980.

2. From "Why Academic Library Instruction?" In *Library Orientation, Ypsilanti, Michigan, 1971*, edited by Sul H. Lee. Ann Arbor: Pierian Press, 1972.

3. From the editorial, *"Pilgrim's Progress"* and *"The Bible,"* page 831 of *Library Journal* 106(8) for April 15, 1981.

4. From Dennis Dickinson's article, "Library Literacy: Who? When? Where?" in *Library Journal* 106(8) for April 15, 1981.

INTRODUCTION AND WELCOME

Morell D. Boone
Director
Eastern Michigan University Library

GOOD MORNING!

It is my pleasure to welcome you to the campus of Eastern Michigan University twice this morning.

The first welcome is by way of introducing our President, Dr. John W. Porter. Dr. Porter became the seventeenth President of Eastern Michigan University in September of 1979. He came to Eastern from our State Capitol where he had served for ten years as Michigan's Superintendent of Public Instruction.

It is very fitting that Dr. Porter officially opens this Eleventh Annual Library Instruction Conference on Teaching Library Use Competence: Bridging the Gap from High School to College. As head of Michigan's Department of Education, he implemented numerous education programs and was recognized for his outstanding contributions in the pursuit of educational excellence. Among his accomplishments were the "Six Step Accountability Model," which he designed, and the concept of the "Educational Health Check-up." During President Porter's two years at Eastern, he has continued to be deeply committed to the pursuit of educational excellence. He has brought to our University a renewed emphasis on putting the students' learning experiences before all else. His vast reservoir of educational experiences and personal integrity has earned him a reputation among the faculty and students as a knowledgeable, fair and dynamic leader.

. . . I'm back for my second and final welcome. This welcome is mine by way of a few personal words of greeting as the recently-appointed Director of Eastern's Center of Educational Resources.

There are four interesting (I hope) ironies that come to mind as I stand before you this morning. The first occurred in the beginning of my academic library career in 1969 when I was one of the original group of New York State college librarians to actively participate in a five–member committee on bibliographic instruction within the New York State Library Association. The irony is that two of the other members were John Lubans and Art Young. In Library Instruction circles they are well known today and I am not -- but I am greeting you – they are not.

The second irony developed when Carolyn Kirkendall asked me to do the honors today, and I had to say that I might not be able to do so because I might be on my way to Africa. The irony is that when I asked my friend, Bob Wedgeworth, Executive Director of ALA, to speak at a dedication ceremony a few years ago, he said, "I might not be able to do so because I might be on my way to Africa." I thought at the time -- how ostentatious of him! Well, Bob was able to give the speech on a Friday and leave for Africa on Saturday. Seven years later, I'm able to give my welcomes on Thursday and leave for Africa on Sunday.

The third irony happened when I was Dean of Learning Resources at the University of Bridgeport. The Library Director and myself had the need to mount a library skills course for credit in a hurry. The specific irony is that this time last year we were on the phone with a Carolyn Kirkendall in Ypsilanti, Michigan, trying to glean everything we could about new approaches to library instruction. One year later, I'm with Carolyn welcoming you to Ypsilanti and presently helping to pay for the phone that she used to talk with us and hundreds of other people about library instruction.

The fourth and final irony is that unless some changes are made in the LOEX financial support base, there may not be a Twelfth Annual Library Instruction Conference, or even a LOEX Clearinghouse at Eastern. The fact is that this year's subscriptions have not kept pace with the ever-increasing costs of operation. However, we are optimistic that there will be a conference next year and that LOEX will be at Eastern for many years to come. To insure this, we must have a LOEX Clearinghouse that is supported by its members who receive its services. Now is not the time to go into this in any more detail. Carolyn will be corresponding with you in the near future to offer you an opportunity to help keep LOEX healthy and serving you and your colleagues. We ask you to give this offer your most serious attention. If you have used the Clearinghouse services in the past, or plan to in the future, and if you are pleased with this Conference, we hope that you will join with us in keeping a professional commitment to this important source of information exchange about library instruction.

All ironies aside, you are here today and tomorrow to participate in a vibrant program of information exchange. The campus of Eastern Michigan is at your disposal. The staffs of the Library and other units of the CER extend their welcome. If there is anything that we can do to help your stay be more productive, please do not hesitate to call upon us.

LOEX and the Division of Continuing Education have arranged an outstanding roster of speakers and discussion leaders. I know that you are anxious to get started. In order to facilitate this, I will now turn the podium over to Carolyn Kirkendall, the Director of the LOEX Clearinghouse.

HELPING STUDENTS MAKE THE TRANSITION: A STUDY

Joyce A. Merriam
University of Massachusetts--Amherst

Just this past week, as I was leaving the library for the day, I happened to overhear the remarks of one young undergraduate to another, as the two moved slowly toward the Reference Room. One was saying, in a lightly sarcastic tone, "Am I looking forward to this! I have to find information for my paper, and I haven't a *clue* as to how to begin!"

I turned quickly to see if the student was going to ask for help at the Reference Desk. She was, so I continued on my way, knowing that my colleague at the desk was excellent at helping even the "no clue" student learn to articulate the nature of his or her needs.

What stuck in my mind, though, were the remarks this student had made before she asked for help at the Reference Desk. It was clear that she expected "a hard time." She knew that she would flounder without help, but how much help could she reasonably expect to get? Could she get by on what she already knew about libraries plus some suggestions and a moderate amount of help from a reference librarian?

To the questions I imagined this student had in her mind, I added some others. Had this student ever been exposed to a library instruction program in the past, somewhere along the lines in grades K--12? Had she ever used a card catalog and *Readers' Guide* to locate materials? If so, had that been just a one-time experience, light-years away, when she was a sophomore in high school? How different was her current research problem from the one(s) she had encountered in the past? Would she need to use types of materials or formats (such as microfiche) which she had never used before?

BACKGROUND OF 1979 STUDY

Questions like these, relating to the current level of skill possessed by students entering the University of Massachusetts at Amherst, were what prompted me in 1979 to study existing library instruction programs in secondary schools throughout Massachusetts, with emphasis on the thirty school systems identified by our Admissions Office as feeder schools, or primary sources of students for our campus.[1] I planned to share with the school librarians concerns of the University Library's Instruction Program relating to those levels of skill and to acquaint them with the status of our library program and with its goal.

My major objective was to find ways of helping students make the transition from high school to academic library. I suspected that lack of communication between high school and academic librarians on this subject had resulted in lost opportunities for us all to develop more relevant instructional services for the college-bound student as well as for the college freshman.

DESCRIPTION OF PROJECT

I selected forty high schools to visit while I was on sabbatical leave between January and June, 1979. Of the forty high schools I visited, thirty-one were feeder schools for the University. All of these were large, regional high schools with student enrollments ranging from 1500–1800 students. The other schools visited were smaller, one with an enrollment of only 500. One was a private, independent school.

Following my visits to individual school libraries, I compiled folders containing information on each one, including a "profile sheet" summarizing notes I had taken at the time of my visit. Points of similarity and difference that would be apparent to students coming from the school library setting to the University Library system were noted. (For a summary of these points, see Appendix 1.)

In most cases, the profile sheets included statistics on the school's enrollment; number of graduates currently at UMass,; size of the print and non-print collection; number of librarians and support staff; number of current periodical subscriptions; availability of microtext material, vertical files, photocopy machines; type of card catalog (divided or dictionary arrangement); classification system used; and a brief description of the library orientation and instruction program offered to all (or to most) students.

Also included in the folders were copies of self-designed library instruction materials that individual librarians were willing to give me to help provide a better picture of library activities at a particular school. I had prepared folders containing similar kinds of information about the University Library to leave with the librarians I visited. Since then, I've been told by several of those librarians that they have used materials from my kit with seniors, to draw attention to similarities and differences between school and academic library resources.

The following kinds of materials were donated to me by the school librarians: pretests, exercise sheets, information sheets for teachers and students on the basic library tools such as the card catalog and *Readers' Guide*; handouts outlining suggested search strategies, guidelines for library instruction programs K--12 (available in a few school systems only), information packages designed for students working on term papers, periodical subscription lists, etc.

The information gathered together in these folders has enabled me and my colleagues in the Reference Department to better understand and appreciate the many factors which contribute to individual student attitudes and understandings about libraries before they come to the University as freshmen. The information about instruction programs at particular schools has been of special interest, because it has enabled us to see more clearly why students who have attended certain schools are likely to have achieved greater competency in the use of basic library tools and techniques for information retrieval than have students from other schools which, at present, have not developed programs which prepare sizeable numbers of students for purposeful use of libraries to support curricular objectives.

One positive outgrowth of my 1979 project was the University Library's first "Library Instruction Colloquium," held in Amherst on June 1, 1979. School librarians I had visited were invited to visit us: (1) to form an impression of the University Library as it might be seen by freshmen coming from the school library setting; (2) to exchange ideas and samples of instructional materials useful for suggesting changes in our instructional program.

The colloquium was a successful one, enabling us all to receive fresh insights with respect to the relative status of our individual instruction programs. Hopefully, we can get together again, in the not too distant future, to continue our efforts to coordinate our respective instructional programs. When we meet again, we may find that "Proposition 2½," which was not foreseen in 1979, has had both good and bad effects: bad in that money for library staff and materials has been seriously curtailed; good in that in some school systems, thought may be given to concentrating elementary library skills training in the elementary schools, freeing up high school librarians for instruction in more advanced aspects of library use.

In some school systems, remaining librarians may have to teach teachers to teach library skills, since there won't be enough librarians to handle the task of teaching the students! With proper planning, coordination and cooperation on the part of librarians and teachers, this could have positive results, since it would divide up responsibility for introducing course-related skills among departments. Unfortunately, it would seem that positive effects of "Proposition 2½" would be possible only in systems already firmly committed to the support of library instruction.

SURVEY FINDINGS

I'd like to refer now to my 1979 survey findings relating to existing library instruction programs in the high schools and at the University, since these findings can serve as a base for thinking and discussion for the rest of the program.

The High School Programs

I was encouraged to find all of the secondary school librarians I visited attempting to provide at least minimal amounts of library orientation and instruction to all students. Only a very few of the school librarians I interviewed felt so constrained by circumstances that they despaired of doing much more than providing small numbers of students with just a quick orientation to the library/media center itself. Because of lack of administrative and faculty support, or staff shortages, they did little in the way of course-related library instruction. Most library instruction at these schools, therefore, took place on a one-to-one basis, involving only those students who asked for assistance when they came to the library.

The "typical" basic library orientation and instruction program, however, was of this nature: (1) all freshman English classes (or sophomore, if a 3-year school) would be brought to the library by their teachers for one to two class periods for orientation to the physical arrangement of the library, its services, rules, and general procedures for use; (2) fundamentals relating to use of the card catalog and *Readers' Guide* would be reviewed; (3) in-class exercises and/or follow-up assignments would be given so that students could practice application of certain learned information immediately; (4) additional follow-up assignments made by the English Department would require students to make use of at least some library materials and some library skills for a specific course-related purpose.

In the typical program, one class period would often be devoted to library orientation and related activities. A second class period would be devoted to basic instruction in the use of two of the school library's major access tools, the card catalog and *Readers' Guide*. In a few schools, three or more class periods would be set aside for these purposes, to allow the time realistically needed for pre-testing, more thorough instruction, individual help, and completion of in-class exercises designed to reinforce course-related library skills.

4

At all high schools I visited, opportunities for many students to master basic library-related concepts and skills did exist. In practice, however, few students were taking advantage of these opportunities -- not because the library collections were inadequate to support a strong program of basic library instruction (most collections were excellent), not because the librarians were disinterested (on the contrary, librarians were concerned with finding ways to improve and expand their instructional programs), but because literature searching was not sufficiently integrated with the course curriculum at most schools to make mastery of basic library skills seem relevant to more than small numbers of students.

The University Program

Ideally, the program of basic library instruction at the University would reach all freshmen, making up for any previous lack of preparation In at least the basic skills and concepts. It might even take students beyond the basics, to stimulate interest in using the research collection for independent study.

Unfortunately, the aims of the university's library instruction program for freshmen are quite limited and, as a result, the overwhelming majority of freshmen on campus rely heavily on library skills acquired earlier in grades K--12. This situation is not unique to the University of Massachusetts. The fact is that relatively few students on any college campus receive formal training in the use of libraries.

At the University, general library instruction sessions may be requested by instructors in the freshman Rhetoric (English Composition) program. These sessions typically involve *a single class period*, which means that limited amounts of basic material must be presented selectively to provide information needed by the poorly prepared as well as the better prepared student. For a number of reasons, including major difficulties in scheduling library sessions for so many students and in finding staff time to devote to this kind of instruction, only about 30% of more than 4,300 freshmen taking Rhetoric receive even this amount of group instruction and review of library "basics."

Approximately 30% of the freshman class take the Library's general orientation tour, to acquaint them with facilities and services. Attendance for the tour is voluntary. We do not know how many of the 30% taking the tour are later among the 30% receiving a review of basic skills through the Rhetoric program but obviously, there are large numbers of freshmen who are not reached at all through the University's efforts to provide library instruction for in-coming students. They must, therefore, be attempting to adapt understand-

5

ings and skills acquired in the school library to the new situations they encounter in the academic library.

One finding of particular interest to me was that the typical program of basic library orientation and instruction in the high schools was almost identical to the one presented to freshmen at the University. My pre-sabbatical suspicions about this were confirmed, and I am now convinced that we at the University should be making special efforts to give new emphases to the orientation and instruction program for freshmen here. Basic library instruction at the University level need not appear to freshmen to be "just a review of things learned about years ago."

Before concluding with recommendations for changes needed in our instructional programs, I'd like to make some further general observations about library instruction.

GENERAL OBSERVATIONS RELATING TO LIBRARY INSTRUCTION

As librarians, we should not be surprised to find that students who come to college ignorant of the nature and organization of an academic collection and who lack even a working knowledge of its basic tools for access, are likely as college freshmen to become hesitant, superficial users at best, remaining ignorant of many of the practical helps it offers, and blind to the potential for creative use of its research materials. We know that there is a wide unfortunate gap between what is available for use in the academic library and what is needed in the way of instruction to prepare students for making informed use of it.

To help close this gap, students should be learning a sequence of library skills to prepare themselves for personal involvement in information searching. By the time they graduate from high school, they should have acquired positive attitudes toward libraries, have learned to understand the different functions of school and public libraries in society, and have learned general techniques for information searching in them. They should be aware of the transfer value of what they have learned (in relation to the public library and, for the college-bound, to the academic library as well), be aware of the strengths and limitations of their present levels of skill, and know that professionally trained staff will be available in most libraries to help them locate information there.

At the college level, students should have opportunities to learn about the development of the literature related to particular subjects, so that they will understand the need for different search strategies depending on factors ranging from currency of the information needed, to the relative importance of certain types of published materials as media for communication in the professional fields. With the aid of reference librarians, they should develop skills related to literature searching in their chosen fields of study and, realizing that they will not become familiar with literature searching in all fields, know that reference librarians can help them to locate information in these other specialized sources too, when and if shifts in their informational needs require it.

Unfortunately, most students never progress beyond the low level skill in using libraries, because the limited amounts of instruction most receive tend to concentrate on this level, in repetitive, circular fashion. We find that basic library skills must be reviewed at each school level, junior high through college, because of the basic skills are easily forgotten if they are not regularly used to help fulfill needs arising from academic course work. In many of today's schools these needs do not arise often.

At the heart of the problem is the large number of teachers who see no reason to integrate library skills with their classroom instruction. When teachers see no "need" for students to use the library (except as a study hall or as a place to read materials "on reserve"), most students will see no need to use the library either. The result is a standstill in the area of library instruction for large numbers of students. The positive experiences they should have in using a variety of informational resources, so that they learn how to select the right kind of tool for the appropriate purpose simply never occur, even though library resources have been purchased to support the entire curriculum offered at most schools.

Once at the University, the majority of students never receive additional formal instruction in basic library skills. Instead, sizeable numbers of students ask for individual help "as needed" at Reference Desks. Professionally trained librarians, who have advanced degrees not only in library science, but often in subject areas as well, are kept busy providing various kinds of reference assistance, at various levels of complexity, individually, to one student after another. Obviously, this kind of assistance can be very valuable for certain purposes, but it can never be a substitute for a planned program of general library instruction. Teaching basic library concepts and skills to large numbers of students on a one-to-one, haphazard basis is sadly inadequate and inefficient. Inevitably, it does much to create an atmosphere of frustration for reference librarians and students alike.

A further drawback associated with teaching basic skills during brief, one-to-one encounters, is that the circumstances necessitate fragmented, incomplete instruction in those skills. Only those points of information which seem relevant to the immediate question, as posed by the student, are likely to be touched upon.

An additional complication exists as well: few students today know enough about potential sources of recorded information or about possible approaches to information retrieval in libraries to know what kinds of questions to be asking of reference librarians in the first place! Often a reference librarian has more than a little difficulty finding out what a student really needs to know in order to solve his or her problems in locating information. Recognition should be given to the fact that much of this difficulty arises because students have little understanding of the search process, and do not think to supply information that will contribute to a meaningful dialogue in the reference interview. Even a reference librarian who is quite skilled in conducting a reference interview would perform more efficiently and, perhaps better, if the dialogue were not so one-sided.

Lastly, the fact that many students never ask for help at all is of concern to us. Some students realize that their questions relate to basic skills and are too embarrassed to admit needing instruction of this kind. Rather than ask for individual help, they flounder about, wasting time and effort needlessly. Others make a similar mistake but for opposite reasons: they feel that they know enough about library skills already, having learned something about basic tools such as general encyclopedias, the card catalog, and *Readers' Guide* in school, and proceed to apply these limited skills to all new situations encountered at college, not realizing that their knowledge of available resources and their techniques for utilizing them *are* limited. It simply does not occur to them that it might be worthwhile to ask a reference librarian about search strategies appropriate for use in a large collection. They too proceed independently, never "bothering" a reference librarian with questions, never asking for advice, because they are confident they can find "enough" on their own. As a result, relatively few take advantage of the wide range of resources available to them in the academic library.

Undoubtedly, students such as those described above do not fully understand the role of the reference librarian, perhaps having learned only that they can "always ask for help at the Reference Desk," and that they should certainly do so "if they can't find what they want on their own." Some students will respond to this vaguely described offer of assistance, especially if they are unable to find any information independently. Many others, however, do not respond because the information given to them about reference service has been inadequate. It has not focused attention on the specialized nature of reference work, or given examples of specific kinds of assistance that can be best provided by a professionally trained reference librarian.

RECOMMENDATIONS

Changes in our programs of library instruction are necessary if we are to bring about desirable changes in the way students use libraries. I make the following recommendations in the hope that they will suggest changes that can be made within individual schools and school systems to improve programs of library instruction for students.

1. All school systems that have not already done so should take steps to develop a planned, sequential program of library/media skills instruction K--12.[2]

2. School librarians should be alert to opportunities to teach students the transfer value of library skills being learned (i.e., in relation to the public library and, for the college-bound, the academic library as well). Students should understand the different purposes served by the public and academic libraries, since they will have access to both types.

3. School librarians should consider pre-testing of college-preparatory students for understanding of library-related concepts and proficiency in library skills that have transfer value for college use, following up with a workshop for students in need of improvement.[3]

4. Principals and librarians should encourage more teachers to integrate literature searching with their curriculum. Students will have little opportunity to become proficient in even the basic skills if they are "needed" once, twice, or perhaps not at all after completion of initial library orientation and instruction exercises. Without proficiency in the basic skills, it is unlikely that they will be able to make effective use of their library during their school years, the time when for many, learning procedures and course-related materials will be of greatest use -- not only for achieving academic success, but for preparing themselves for independence in research.

5. Librarians/media specialists should think of ways that we as professionals could influence Schools of Education to better prepare prospective teachers for integrating library and media skills with their classroom instruction. (Should courses in Curriculum Development include units on integrating library/media skills with the curriculum? Should teachers be given an opportunity to take continuing education workshops on these subjects for credit?)

6. School librarians should help college-bound students to learn the value of a search strategy as a technique for retrieving needed information from relevant library resources. Search

strategy is one of the most important library skills to be learned. Help them to understand that similar, but more specialized search strategies will often be more appropriate for use in the larger academic library. Inform them that as college freshmen they will be expected to seek the assistance of reference librarians in developing the search strategy that correlates best with the academic library collection and their chosen topics for research.

7. School librarians should visit nearby college and university libraries to see these libraries as they would be seen through the eyes of a freshman. School librarians should then be alert to opportunities to develop in college-bound students more sophisticated expectations about the academic library. Impress upon them the fact that learning to use the library is a continuing process.

8. Reference librarians at colleges and universities should become informed about library instruction programs in secondary schools, to increase their sensitivity to unexpressed needs of freshmen in relation to library orientation and instruction programs offered on their own campuses.

9. Reference librarians at colleges and universities should refocus the basic instruction given to freshmen relating to use of the card catalog and *Readers' Guide*, to take into account the manner and circumstances in which those tools would have been used in the high school library as opposed to the somewhat different ways in which they should be used, at more advanced levels, in academic libraries. Emphasize the wider range of resources and finding aids available in the academic library.

10. School and academic librarians should work together to develop programs that help students make the transition from high school to academic library.

Ultimately, the success of our library instruction programs will be dependent upon strong administrative support, plus the cooperation of teachers and librarians in planning together for a library skills program which is of real benefit to students. Further advances in library instruction will be slow in coming unless administrators and teachers can be made to recognize the need for them and accept their share of the responsibility for seeing that they occur.

NOTES

1. Merriam, Joyce. *Helping Students Make the Transition from High School to Academic Library; a Report on a Study of Selected Library Instruction Programs in Massachusetts.* 1979. (ERIC

Document ED 176 783). Much of the text of this paper is taken directly from that earlier report.

2. Possibly a prototype program could be developed by a committee for the use of any interested school system. Several school systems, including Braintree and Natick, Mass., have guidelines for development of library skills K--12 which could serve as useful models for study.

3. Freshmen at Andover High School who do poorly on a library-skills pre-test are contacted by library/media specialists at the school and given individual help as needed to achieve basic levels of competency. A special program of this sort could be developed for college-bound students also.

Comparison Chart

	High School Library/Media Centers Visited	University Library
1. Size of print collection	6,000–40,000 vols. (20,000 vols. common at the feeder schools).	Over 2 million vols.
2. A–V materials	Considerable software and hardware available for student use.	Little A–V material available for student use except for Music Dept. phonorecords and material selected for reserve or classroom use by faculty.
3. Card catalog	Usually a small dictionary catalog; a few of the larger collections had divided catalogs.	Large divided catalog (author/title, subject).
4. Classification system used	Dewey Decimal Classification (with only one exception: Brockton High uses Library of Congress).	Library of Congress Classification. (UMass freshmen need instruction in reading call numbers using this system).
5. Microtext materials	Few. Most libraries had a few periodical backfiles on microfilm, and some fiche. (Exception: Brockton High had a fairly sizeable microtext collection).	Over 25% of the entire collection is in microform.
6. Fiction	Shelved as a separate collection, arranged alphabetically by surname of author.	Shelved according to L.C. classification within the main collection.
7. Paperbacks	Most had separate, attractive collections of current titles for circulation.	No separate collection of paperbacks. These are generally not acquired unless the cloth edition is unavailable.
8. Periodicals	Subscription to 100–150 current titles is common. Hard copy backfiles usually not retained for more than 3–5 yrs.	Subscription to approx. 14,000 current serial titles. Backfiles of 18th, 19th, 20th century periodicals are available.
9. Periodical indexes	Usually *Readers' Guide* only. A few had *RG* 1890–date plus 2–3 other indexes.	Many different periodical indexes available, most focusing on the journal literature of particular disciplines.
10. Basic orientation & instruction	Reached nearly all freshmen; attendance was required in most schools.	Attendance for orientation tours is voluntary; approx. 30% of students attend. Approx. 30% of students enrolled in the Rhetoric Program receive some instruction at a general session.

LEARNING FROM OUR MISTAKES

Mary Biggs
University of Chicago Graduate Library School

I seem to be here today as an expert on mistakes, which I guess is appropriate. If I am an expert on anything regarding library instruction, mistakes are probably it. Because I made them. Since I have been away from the practice of library instruction at the University of Evansville for a year and a half now,[1] they no longer haunt my dreams or my daytime thoughts, but I do cringe occasionally at some memories: At, for example, the over-sophisticated research tool I introduced to a group of bewildered eighteen-year-olds: I quickly recognized my mistake, but I couldn't think what to do with the book. It wouldn't fit in my *pocket*: it was as fat as it was sophisticated; and I was still as unsure of myself as I was ambitious.

Or the times I thought I had communicated with a professor, and hadn't, and misprepared miserably. Not to mention the stories that fell flat; the examples that raised more questions than they resolved; the media presentation that dazzled without enlightening, and robbed me of valuable time; the occasions when I failed to captivate, failed to motivate, and should have, *could* have with better planning. Each of these moments returns like a song, perhaps more like an LSD flashback, and again, though it now can do no practical good, I find myself analyzing why a particular plan, or method, or phrase, did not work. I think the reason we agonize over our failures, minute as they are on a cosmic scale, is because they reflect on us so little. No one really knows what we do wrong, or at least how wrong it is. Professors are usually satisfied with our services, or are dissatisfied for the wrong reasons. So when we fail, we fail the students, no one else, and perhaps first-year students, who are the neediest and least secure, most of all. Nobody blows a whistle on us, and the silence can be maddening.

I want to add that I did have a few successes as well, and in any case, since I left Evansville things there are no doubt looking up. But still, I will guess that I am not the only mistake expert in bibliographic instruction, though I have precious little evidence to support that conjecture. The library literature of the subject radiates success. With a few notable exceptions,[2] every program reported is a smash, every lecture a revelation, every new technique a pedagogical breakthrough, every day in the librarian's life pregnant with joy and reward.

I think it's time to get honest.

Mistakes are not bad things; they're good. If we don't make them, we're not moving. But I see real barriers against identifying our errors accurately and learning from them, and we build the barriers higher with each passing year. Those barriers are founded in our isolation. Yes, busy as we are, crowded as we sometimes feel, we are isolated -- from our students, from our colleagues in other libraries, and even from the effects of our own programs, our own individual efforts. Most of us were in touch once, at least with what *we* were doing. Probably some of us still are. But I am convinced that many instructional programs now proceed principally of their own inertia -- running in the same track, maybe running too fast, standardized, routinized, self-justifying -- like any other library practice which has moved from an innovation to an everyday service.

First of all, and most especially in the case of freshmen, we have little sense of the student mind. I realize that to journey into an eighteen-year-old psyche is neither possible nor particularly appealing. We may suspect it would be a descent into chaos that would discourage us entirely. What we can do is try to understand the background students bring with them into our domain. This necessitates understanding the high school. Although high schools within travelling distance usually will not represent all those which our freshmen have attended, they can offer us a better perspective than most academic librarians now have. Before an instructional program is planned, or failing that, before a planned program is implemented, or failing that as well, after we are knee-deep in misconceptions and wrongheaded practices, we should be out in the field visiting high schools, studying their libraries and media centers, using their collections to do research on typical undergraduate topics. We should be talking seriously and at length with high school librarians, media specialists, and teachers of English and other subjects. We should be observing high school students in their libraries. And if high school library instruction is performed, we should listen in on it and review its products. In some cases, especially when we work in colleges that draw most of their students from specific localities, we can work out alliances and cooperative programs with our counterparts in the high schools. At the very least, if we study several schools, we will be able to generalize about the typical pre-college library experience of our freshmen. Reading the literature of school librarianship can also help, although it shares the unrepresentativeness and sometimes unwarranted optimism of other library literature. Nonetheless, more and more is being printed about school library instruction, and much of it may be more pertinent to our work with freshmen than material written by academicians.

Probably some college librarians are doing the very things I suggest, or better-conceived, more aggressive and imaginative versions of them, and to those librarians I doff my hat. I confess that during my years in Evansville, I never set foot in a high school library, though my colleagues and I welcomed high school classes into ours. That is, of course, an obvious and important gesture, although I have been told by a frustrated high school librarian that not all academic libraries are willing to make it. Such visits can help forge links with the high schools, but they give us only slight indications for the direction of our freshman programs and usually depend upon the initiative of high school personnel, who have even more problems, more tasks, and less time to tangle with them than we have.

I am certain that if we formulate our plans while sitting aloof in academe, we are not going to reach our younger students. I experience a minor cringe when I recall that my reports from Evansville for the NEH (National Endowment for the Humanities) usually included tables showing annual student head counts and, in my text, I occasionally referred to those heads as numbers of students "reached." When *I* was in high school, there was a phrase in common use by those of us who thought we were cool. An acquaintance would be telling her sad story about a cruel parent or lost love, and we would say sarcastically, "I feel for you, but I don't reach you." We librarians, I think, often do the same, *literally*, in our contacts with freshman students. We are feeling for them, but too rarely reaching them, and when we do reach them, we must question how successfully and enduringly we touch them. (That sounds more carnal than I had intended, and I think I'll drop the metaphor.)

I have mentioned a few things I believe we should do in order to enter our students' experience; many other things can be done also. At Evansville, for example, we took turns sitting with the students during our colleagues' presentations, although tight schedules prevented us from doing it often enough. Among the many values of this practice was the chance to draw closer to the student perspective. Of course, it was very imperfect, very partial, we remained librarians, not students, but I recommend that everyone do it and try to follow what is being said; try to take notes; find out if one *must* try to stay interested. And watch the students. The same classroom, the same class, is a different world when seen from the middle of the room or the end of the table, facing in the opposite direction. I also tried to plant more authentic reactors in the group:

genuine students who would experience instruction as students and could report their frank responses back to me. Library student workers can be used in this way; such service is every bit as helpful and justifiable as card-filing or book-shelving. Better yet, perhaps, library-naive student reactors can be recruited in a variety of ways. None of this feedback is, of course, "scientific." No one can perceive instruction precisely as the truly involved student perceives it, and no two perceptions will be identical. But useful, honest observations can be derived in this manner, and probed, and clarified, in ways which are not so easy when coercion, impending assignments, and hovering grades construct a different dynamic.

The kinds of studies and measures I have proposed are neither as quantifiable nor as easy as scoring objective tests, nor are they sufficient, but they can give us some sense of how we and our environment look and feel to the new student. We forget how complex our libraries are, how difficult and esoteric our wealth of professional knowledge really is. We take too much for granted. One of my first instructional efforts involved a careful explanation of periodical indexes to a group of brand new freshmen. I thought at the time that it was an exceptional student, an exceptionally dull oaf, to be exact, who asked me, after forty exhausting minutes of explanation, "What's a periodical?" Experience soon taught me that he was probably a very average new student. I went back to the drawing board. Still, it took me a long time, inexcusably long, to understand that freshman remarks like the following are not compliments, but devastating critiques: "You really covered *everything*!;" I never knew there was *so much* in the library;" "How did you ever *learn* all that?;" "That was great; you taught us an awful lot!" (emphasis on either the "awful" or the "lot" is a dead giveaway). To the extent that we inspire awe, we stretch the distance between our students and our libraries.

We are isolated not only from new students and the schools which send them to us, but from our colleagues in other academic institutions. Many of us don't believe that. We have, after all, three well-established and much-travelled avenues of contact: workshops, meetings, and conferences, like this one; consultancies; and yards, acres, of library literature. While at Evansville, I jogged religiously down these avenues, and I do mean down. I also arranged visits to a few nearby campuses. I talked, and talked, and talked, with other public services librarians. And I learned an amazing and initially chastening thing: nobody but I was doing anything wrong! Frank admissions of problems and serious analyses of existing programs, analyses from the inside, that is, by program practitioners, were so rare in conversation that when they occurred, the confessing deviant was regarded with astonishment and pity. Those of us who had programs well in place, especially programs sanctified and nourished by funding agencies, withdrew into defensive postures. Actual camps could and can be identified: the pro-multimedia group versus the print traditionalists; the workbook authors versus the individualized-learning advocates; the testers versus the anti-testers; the course-integrators versus the separate-coursepersons. At least until recently, there even remained a few hardy holdouts for the old-fashioned tour. I consider them crazy but brave. Semantics became significant. At a workshop, a distinguished figure in bibliographic instruction declared that the type of handout I had developed was not a handout at all, but a workbook. As a dedicated anti-workbooker, I bristled at this and pronounced it indeed a handout. In short, we locked horns, and any discussion of the merits or demerits of my materials was impaled on them.

The literature also teems with "how-we-do-it-good"; I have contributed, and am now contributing, a little of it myself. And much of this is useful to a point: the point where you need to know how good they really do it. Ultimately, and as a whole, these articles are frustrating and untrustworthy, as I learned when a few acclaimed practices were put into motion at Evansville and either flopped or yielded too little in exchange for their demands. Did I miss something? Did fault lie with the authors or with me? Or were they good ideas simply not transportable to my particular environment? I wish now I had studied each little flop and reported it; I wish there were a "how-we-did-it-bad" tradition. I long for critical case studies and symposia. I would like to hear go-for-the-jugular panels of reactors at conferences, and tough, jagged, freely disrespectful questioning sessions after speeches.[3] (I realize I am asking for trouble.) I recall a LOEX conference of a few years ago when one speaker advocated a teaching method that struck me as incredibly stupid. In the small-group discussion which followed, and at which the speaker was not present, we all chuckled and chortled and deplored and denigrated, slapped our knees and each other's backs, felt delightfully superior, and went on to other matters. What good did that do? Why not confront the speaker? Perhaps he could have met our criticisms and revolutionized our thinking; perhaps some modified technique clearly preferable to any of our individual practices would have emerged from a verbal free-for-all. I doubt it: I still think his notion was incredibly stupid. But the point is, no time was scheduled when such an exchange could occur. Had it been, the exchange would still have been unlikely, because in general librarians are entirely too polite, too gentle with each other and themselves. But undue kindliness is a whole other problem, a whole other paper (one which I would be delighted to write!).

Enlightening as errors may be, a battery of reasons prevents our sharing them. Who wants to be known as the librarian who is always messing up at Evansville? Who will get a promotion or a better job on the strength of a series of articles documenting blunders? What funding agency or college president or even library director would be favorably impressed by our ability to identify and analyze mistakes? They want happy endings, not hassles. The entire system in which we operate rewards success, so we are successful, or convince ourselves that we are, or keep quiet. Informally, at least, this can change. True sharing can be accomplished in many ways. It is my impression that few instruction librarians spend time at other academic libraries to study tools and techniques, to ask tough questions of each other and themselves, to attend or participate in or conduct teaching sessions. Why don't we? We have time to attend conferences, often from great distances, as witness this gathering. By now, we should be sufficiently self-assured to engage in brainstorming, criticism, self-analysis, experimentation, and change. I speak here not of consultancies, where presumably expert outsiders are paid to come in and tell the presumably inexpert locals what to do -- in the process perhaps imposing an inappropriate scheme on the feckless inexperts. No, I am talking about real peers with shared goals struggling together to resolve problems in attaining them. I am talking about the beautiful, hardy organisms born of cross-fertilization.

Yet too often such cross-fertilization does not occur even in the most obvious, one would think inescapable, manner -- through colleague interaction at the same institution. And this is because we suffer a third type of isolation: from ourselves. Earlier, I advocated attendance at one another's presentations as a way of drawing closer to the student viewpoint; this can also reward the attendee with valuable ideas and the presenter with useful criticism. It is, I would guess, a rare institution at which librarians systematically review and critique each other's pedagogical methods and classroom images, work in teams, create and revise teaching materials as a group, and meet regularly, gloves off, in a quiet place with no patrons or telephones, to talk, argue, reflect, and plan. Mostly, we are too busy and too decorous. Programs develop, slide sets are created, handouts and workbooks are printed. Faculty members say, "Just do what you did last time, it was fine," though last time, they nodded off in the back of the room. Everything works more or less; everyone is busy; the librarians are acquiring a certain facility, a familiarity with and fondness for the track. The director, president, foundation, or government agency is happy, and money continues to flow, or dribble, in.

At one time, such a situation was not unusual and sufficed to satisfy most librarians. But increasingly, in recent years, evaluation fever has gripped at least some of us, and this is good news.[4] For whatever reason – perhaps that nagging sense that we are feeling for but not reaching our students, perhaps greater emphasis on accountability by administrators faced with dwindling funds, perhaps simple restlessness -- we are more concerned with evaluating what we are doing. The idea of this, an honest librarian would think, should be to detect where and how we are falling short, perhaps to reformulate our goals, certainly to restructure our methods, and try to do better. Instead, as I read the literature, I often suspect that our usual motive for evaluating is to prove the high worth of what we are doing, to score political points. Given the constraints under which we work and the history of many existing programs, politics is necessary and even invigorating. But if that is what motivates us, we should not fool ourselves with the word "evaluation," a word which implies system, rigor, time, risk, and tough librarianly hides. Which implies change, if necessary, and readiness to abandon methods that have won our commitment, for which we may even have fought.

Perhaps I don't read enough, I'm sure I don't -- but I see little evidence of that type of evaluation. I do see much reliance on questionnaires and exercises, on pretests and posttests, and a tendency to miscompute and misread statistics or automatically to equate statistically significant results with solid intellectual gains -- an equation which often is false.[5] Testing can be revealing; certainly it yields quantifiable data which can be politically, and even pedagogically, useful. But it must be employed very cautiously, with an eye to its limitations. Pretesting and posttesting are indicative only if properly selected control groups are tested as well. And surely no evaluation technique is meaningful unless it measures that we want our students to *do*. If, for example, we want them to do research intelligently on a given topic, no short-answer test will tell us much. However, two research papers or annotated bibliographies, one prepared before and one after library instruction, may tell us a good deal, at least about short-range learning. Furthermore, we can draw no conclusions about the relative worth of two techniques unless we have used both with comparable groups and evaluated the results, money costs, and student and staff time associated with each technique. Even the most stupendous student performance following use of an impressive slide-tape or movie or computer program cannot in itself prove that instrument preferable to humble mimeoed handouts or, for that matter, to old-fashioned reference service. Every librarian performing bibliographic instruction, but most crucially those who develop or supervise programs, should at minimum be competent in elementary statistics and simple empirical research methods, and should understand the basic principles of learning theory and educational testing. Moreover, this knowledge must be kept fresh through use and updating. A single course completed in

1958 and forgotten by 1959 doesn't count!

Our concern with quality, efficiency, and comparability, along with the maturing of instruction as a service, seem to be leading, perhaps inevitably, toward standardization. There is a plethora, ever growing, of published texts, lessons, examples, and workbooks,[6] of commercially-produced nonprint tools, and, of course, there are LOEX and other sharing mechanisms. These are well enough in themselves; we are too busy to spend time reinventing the wheel. But we must beware of proliferating square wheels, or of rolling, on our round wheels, confidently into quicksand. I truly fear that standardized materials and methods can insulate us from our mistakes and tempt us to institute programs without assessing thoroughly and sensitively our local environments, needs, and proper goals. We may even be deluded that such assessment is unnecessary, that what is good for, say, Leeward Community College[7] is good for us all.

Well, everything I have suggested takes time: building bridges to the high schools; arranging fruitful interactions with students, with colleagues in other libraries and in our own; evaluating; finding mistakes and working to correct them. Who has the time? Who can spend hours in each of a half dozen high schools? Who can worrry about control groups? What library, where, in this straitened decade, can allow its staff time for long bull sessions, mutual observing, soul-searching, reporting, thinking? Time is a scarce commodity, to be sure, but we would better limit our activities and do what we *do* well, than rush hither and yon, "reaching" students, tallying head counts, teaching cheap and easy -- and badly. It is *that* which we cannot afford. We must ask ourselves whether a library that cannot spare its staff time for consultation, planning, and limited travel has any business in formalized bibliographic instruction. For many libraries, the optimal strategy may be to maximize traditional services: to improve reference service, directional graphics, internal arrangement, and circulation and technical procedures, and to select materials more judiciously. We should pull back and ask not, "Is this desirable?" bibliographic instruction, I assert, is, but, "Can we do it well with the resources we have?" If we lack time to detect and rectify mistakes, we can't. And if we can't do it well, we shouldn't do it.

It is popularly said, and presumably believed, that those who ignore history are condemned to repeat it, though this belief doesn't seem to influence public policy. Well, if we ignore our mistakes, we'll repeat them, and if we are kept ignorant of others' mistakes, we'll commit them needlessly. But I am optimistic because I'm convinced that librarians are smarter than politicians. Our efforts should and can be guided by constant, frank discussion, meaningful evaluation, and analysis -- all shorn of sentimental rhetoric. Bibliographic instruction has passed through its infant booster phase, and librarians are groping to realize its great promise. But we cannot do this in isolation; we cannot do it behind barriers. The time is here to break them down, to risk the glare of direct, revealing sunlight on what we are doing. Such light can destroy or heal. I believe we and our service are now strong enough, mature enough, to deflect it to our purposes and flourish.

NOTES

1. For a description of the Evansville program in its earlier phases, see: Mary Biggs and Mark Weber, *Course-Related and Personalized Library Instruction*, 1979, ED 172 724.

2. The most famous exception is, of course, the Monteith College program; see. Patricia B. Knapp, *The Monteith College Library Experiment* (New York: Scarecrow Press, 1966). Edward G. Holley, among others, has also commented on the non-reporting of failures; see: Holley, "Library Instruction: Some Observations from the Past and Some Questions for the Future," *Improving Library Instruction: How to Teach and How to Evaluate*, ed. Carolyn A. Kirkendall (Ann Arbor, Mich.: Pierian Press, 1979).

3. Some symposium-like features have appeared in print, though they usually do not permit direct interaction. Examples include: Carolyn Kirkendall, ed., "Library Instruction: A Column of Opinion," *Journal of Academic Librarianship*, Vol. 2 (March, 1976) -- present; and Cerise Oberman-Soroka, ed., *Proceedings from the 2nd Southeastern Conference on Approaches to Bibliographic Instruction, March 22--23, 1979.* (Charleston, S.C.: College of Charleston Library Associates, 1980). Occasionally conference planners do allow for after-speech discussions and publication of these discussions; see, for example: Ian Malley, ed., *Educating the User: Papers Given at a Two-Day Course Held at The Library Association on 16 and 17 November 1977* (London: Library Association, 1979). This strategy varies in successfulness, of course, depending upon the degree of enlightenment and tough-mindedness of the discussion participants.

4. Among the more thoughtful commentators on evaluation are Richard Hume Werking and James Benson. See: Werking, "The Place of Evaluation in Bibliographic Education," *Proceedings from Southeastern Conference on Approaches to Bibliographic Instruction, March 16--17, 1978*, ed. Cerise Oberman-Soroka

(Charleston, S.C.: Continuing Education Office, College of Charleston, 1978); Werking, "Evaluating Bibliographic Education: A Review and Critique," *Library Trends*, Vol. 29 (Summer, 1980) p. 153--72; and Benson, "Bibliographic Education: A Radical Assessment," *Proceedings from the 2nd Southeastern Conference on Approaches to Bibliographic Instruction, March 22–23*, ed. Cerise Oberman-Soroka (Charleston, S.C.: College of Charleston Library Associates, 1980).

5. Since I cannot here present an exposition of any particular study, it is fairest not to cite those I consider vulnerable. However, other readers have criticized the accuracy and utility of statistical evaluations of bibliographic instruction. See, for example: Linda L. Phillips and E. Ann Raup, "Comparing Methods for Teaching Use of Periodical Indexes," *Journal of Academic Librarianship*, Vol. 4 (January, 1979) p. 420--23, and a critique by Mignon Adams, [letter], *Journal of Academic Librarianship*, Vol. 5 (May, 1978) p. 93--94. See also: Stuart Glogoff, "Using Statistical Tests to Evaluate Library Instruction Sessions," *Journal of Academic Librarianship*, Vol. 4 (January, 1979) p. 438--442, and a critique by Mark Schumacher, [letter], *Journal of Academic Librarianship*, Vol. 5 (May, 1979) p. 92--93. But Phillips, Raup, and Glogoff should perhaps not be singled out; reports of weak statistical and other types of evaluations are not difficult to find in our literature.

6. Among the very many examples are: Floyd M. Cammack, Marri DeCosin, and Norman Roberts, *Community College Library Instruction* (Hamden, Conn.: Linnet Books, 1979); James R. Kennedy, Jr. and Thomas G. Kirk, Jr., eds., "Library Research Guides" Series (Ann Arbor, Mich.: Pierian Press); and the "learning packages" derived from the British Travelling Workshops Experiment and reported in: Colin Harris, Daphne Clark, and Anne Douglas, "The Travelling Workshops Experiment," *Progress in Educating the Library User*, ed. John Lubans, Jr. (New York: R. R. Bowker Co., 1978), and Daphne Clark and Colin Harris, "Can Users Be Instructed by Package? Report: Encouraging," *Library Association Record*, Vol. 80 (June, 1978) p. 279--281.

7. Cammack, DeCosin, and Roberts's book (see footnote 6) deals with a program developed at Leeward Community College.

LIBRARY USER EDUCATION IN SECONDARY SCHOOLS

Ann Irving
Loughborough University: England

> *"People are always blaming their circumstances for what they are. I do not believe in circumstances. The people who get on in this world are the people who get up and look for the circumstances they want, and if they cannot find them, make them."* George Bernard Shaw

Shaw's sentiments echo those of this paper, and also perhaps, of user education itself. We hope that user education offers knowledge and skills which will enable people to handle and manipulate information so that they may indeed look for and make the circumstances they want. The paper which follows illuminates a number of activities and experiences which demonstrate how and why British researchers are creating the circumstances we *all* need if we are to facilitate the development of these skills by library users.

The current status of user education in schools in the United Kingdom could be described as surprising for there has been a great deal of retrenchment from an already vulnerable position. Schools and libraries have suffered financially during the economic recession, but the reductions in spending and support were made in an area where both were already low. The existence of any activity is therefore surprising; the richness of this activity is easily described as amazing! That there are plans for the future is surely astounding, and surely, too, a clear example of what 'looking for and making circumstances' really means.

The aim of this exposition is therefore to examine the current status and future projections of user education in schools, but not as a tabulation of relevant work, rather as a synthesis of relevant work within a comparative framework. By making comparisons between British and American conditions it is possible to consider the shifting approaches of United Kingdom researchers and how these relate to the tertiary sector of education. Some of the different approaches are subtle in both theory and practice, but they are also significant in both application and impact. We seem to be making headway in areas where progress has long been desired: we seem to be creating the circrumstances we want, at last.

How Do We Compare: U.K. and U.S.A.?

American school libraries are viewed with importance by teachers and librarians. The literature on school libraries in the U.S.A. is vast; in Britain it is scarce. Much of it is written by school librarians, of course, and in Britain they are a tiny proportion of our profession: out of 25,000 librarians on the Library Association register, less than 500 are school librarians, yet we have 8,000 secondary schools. The majority of high school students never encounter a librarian during their school years; all students in higher education have access to at least one. It is not surprising, therefore, that school librarians in Britain are not 'high status' members of staff. Too few teachers are even aware of their existence.

With such small numbers of librarians in schools it is rare to find more than one in any school, irrespective of size, number of sites or range of academic work. Clerical help is very rare and much time is spent on the minutiae of library work. When there are so few librarians, who are geogrpahically widely scattered, co-operative purchasing or processing schemes seem impossible to create.

The curriculum in any school is an individually-tailored structure. There is no legislation to dictate what should be taught, except for the 1944 Education Act which insisted on the inclusion of religious education, the only compulsory course in Britain. External pressures have, however, resulted in a consensus curriculum. Parents, employers and higher education exert an influence which results in several 'core' elements in the curriculum, e.g. English and Mathematics. This autonomy adds to the librarian's difficulties, for co-operation is made difficult by such flexibility, and the prospect of area or national library media skills programmes, so common in the U.S.A., is intangible to most U.K. school librarians.

A further complication arises from their education and training. U.S.A. school librarians are dually-qualified, which offers the prospect of equal status, pay and working conditions. Such people are increasing in the U.K., but opportunities are few and the standards of qualification available are variable. Where dual-qualification exists it is usually acquired at postgraduate level, the graduate student entering either librarianship or teaching after a first degree in another academic discipline, and then acquiring another postgraduate qualification in order to gain recognition from both professions. Unlike American school librarians, dually-qualified librarians in the U.K.

are usually expected to teach a 'proper subject' (e.g. English or history), limiting their time for library work to perhaps an hour or two per week. User education thus becomes only one of many neglected activites. Perhaps its existence at all despite such circumstances, is surprising, amazing *and* astounding?

Do We Have Anything in Common?

We share many similar experiences, particularly in user education. Many are also shared by colleagues in higher education. Gaining faculty co-operation has always proved difficult, although the situation is less gloomy than before. Librarians, being usually or often the sole representative of their profession in a school, feel isolated and undervalued by teaching colleagues. We have all wrestled with the problem of evaluation in the search for justification of user education. Jo Anne Nordling eloquently exposes another common problem:

> "Even in a school system that provides elementary librarians, librarians who work hard at their jobs, too many students enter high school unable to utilize the library as a working tool for their personal and academic needs. As one high school teacher said, 'The poor students know how to copy out of the encyclopedia; the good students know how to use the *Readers' Guide*, look up books in the card catalog, and copy out of the encyclopedia."[1]

Mindless copying is surely the product of misunderstanding of the purpose of library use and an example of one of the gaps in user education shared by librarians on both sides of the Atlantic Ocean. Also absent is a real appreciation for student perceptions and views, not only about school libraries but also about the nature of school itself, as manifested by the series of assignments which compose, in the student's view, the experience of school education.

It is at this point that the practices of those concerned with user education in schools begin to diverge between our two nations. The lack of provision, finance, support and manpower in U.K. schools has necessitated the creation of different circumstances. The 'traditional' approaches of library orientation and bibliographic instruction cannot be contemplated. The research and practice has necessarily shifted away from what John Lubans referred to as:

> " . . . . . . what librarians think library users ought to know."[2]

because of the circumstances in which librarians and students, found themselves after almost one hundred years of library instruction theory and practice reported in the literature.[3]

Divergence

Frances drew attention to the need for divergence many years ago:

"In the viewpoint of many school librarians the mere process of locating and finding materials in the library holds little intellectual benefit for students, and time thus spent is generally wasted time. The many processes involved in what students do with materials -- evaluation, synthesis, reflection, thinking, appreciation, or whatever -- are the important factors, not the searching, locating, and assembling of materials."[4]

Michael Brittain made a similar distinction between,
". . . instruction in the use of libraries and bibliographical tools on the one hand, and instruction in the use of information on the other. When most people talk about user or library instruction they are referring to the former."[5]

Both writers emphasize the *use* of information rather than its location and retrieval and it is in dealing with the skills for using information that the divergence is most apparent. The process of information use is directly related to, and focussed on, the classroom, where students and teachers spend much of their time together. Classrooms are where school assignments are generated and through these, the notion of skills which facilitate their completion. Frances Henne argued for an analysis of all assignments as a means for indicating where the library instruction program might be integrated with the curriculum; where teachers might be involved with planning instruction. Recent work[6] from a working group sponsored by the Schools Council and the British Library also argues for an analysis of assignments, but for the analysis to be made by teachers so that librarians might be involved in the planning of teaching. A subtle but significant difference.

The Information Skills in the Curriclm Research Unit[7] is currently using the 'Information skills curriculum' produced by the British Library/Schools Council working group as a guide to developing awareness in the minds of teachers and students of the range and nature of assignment skills. The working group report also contains a workship for teachers which creates for them circumstances which enable them to reflect on their existing assignments by means of the 'Information skills curriculum' framework. The workshop employs a method which is becoming increasingly more popular in Britain and which was originally developed by Graham Gibbs[8], then based at the Open University. The method is essentially one of reflection -- of existing study methods, attitudes and behaviour -- and works equally well with teachers and students. Each exercise in the manual examines one or more common study problems and by a process of reflection, sharing experiences, and discussion, workshop participants uncover a range of strategies for using information. When teachers take part in the workshops, very little instruction is necessary: problems and solutions are 'discovered' and therefore rather more effectively learned.

When coupled with the 'Information skills curriculum' the approach developed by Gibbs has proved highly effective in changing the perceptions, attitudes and behaviour of teachers. Naturally, such a workshop requires more than a few participants; interdisciplinary groups of teachers enter into a stage of realisation which has never been induced by reading research reports or listening to library and information personnel. Teachers leave the workshops *knowing* why their assignments are not satisfactorily completed by students; *knowing* why library materials are mis-used; *knowing* where intervention or instruction on the use of information (as well as its location and retrieval) is needed; and *knowing* who can best advise them on such matters.

The method also 'teaches' about itself; participants learn of its effectiveness as a means for helping students learn how to learn, through reflecting experiences back to individuals, and out to the rest of the group.

Experience is the keyword for the 'Teaching of Study Skills' project based at the National Foundation for Educational Research[9]. When students are consulted about their study methods they are surprisingly articulate. Teachers are asked to provide students' notes, for example, and in discussion they discern the important effects of their teaching methods upon student learning. Perhaps this is enough to jolt the teacher into a re-appraisal of her teaching and assignment-setting, and consequently lead her into designing more appropriate tasks for developing the skills for using information; certainly this project is bringing them into the view of those who have for too long failed to perceive them, despite the widely-reported work of Edward de Bono and Tony Buzan:

Buzan refers to the information and publication explosions and the relative neglect of the individual's ability to handle and study it:

"If he is ever to cope with the situation he must learn not more 'hard facts' but new ways of handling and studying the information – new ways of using his natural abilities to learn, think, recall, create, and solve problems".[10]

Whilst de Bono argues for the teaching of thinking as a skill on the assumptions that it can be improved, and that there can be "a uniformity of reaction at a basic thinking level across wide ranges of age, ability and interest."[11] Later de Bono makes a statement which is quite significant for librarians engaged in user education:

"It is best to remember that information is no substitute for thinking and that thinking is no substitute for information. There is a need for both."

The reason why this is so significant is that it contains a silent warning about the mere retrieval of information, which has no power or meaning without the skills needed for its use. This is where the research so far mentioned has begun; with the major thinking or cognitive skills which must be developed before a library can begin to be used intelligently or effectively or efficiently. And before reaching the school library, students have been sitting in class-rooms . . . with their teachers. Terry Brake, whose 'Need to Know' project[12] provided many insights into how students viewed informa-tion concepts, skills and instruction, reduces the idea of use to one simple sentence:

"I would rather a pupil could effectively gain access into, and derive meaning from one source, than that she could find the titles of three hundred."[13]

This is precisely where we are aiming, and the course is through teachers rather than librarians. Thus we emphasize the role of the librarian as an educator of teachers, not users – another significant divergence, although the idea is not a new one, as John Lubans notes:

"In our missionary-like zeal, we appear to be convincing the converted and *not* the great unwashed of users/misusers/non-users, including the key individual that possesses the greatest ability to make changes in the use of libraries: the teacher."[14]

Teachers do not know how to use libraries, as both American and British researchers have shown[15] and because of the constraints outlined earlier in this paper we have ceased to believe that circum-stances can be changed by continuing to direct effort, energy and scarce manpower resources towards *student* user education. Teacher cdcuation is the current aim, and if this cannot be achieved entirely by means of in-service workshops, it is at least encouraged by a form of 'education by embarrassment' -- publicity for school libraries, information and study skills in strategic places at strategic times (for example, in evidence submitted to the Select Committee on Education, Science and Arts of the House of Commons).[16] Although the financial picture remains a dismal one for school libraries, there are brighter horizons for the work described as 'information skills' and for the work being carried out with and for teachers.

Projections: Where Next?

Some gaps in our knowledge of how students and teachers use libraries and information are currently being filled. Laurence Stenhouse is directing research into library access, use and user education in academic sixth forms (for 17–18 year old students)[17] which involves the compilation of detailed case records of interviews with school management teams, library staff, teachers, and students. Among the project aims are several which indicate the direction of British thinking:

"to draw implications for teaching in the presence of libraries and for user education.

"to make recommendations for curriculum development in user education at sixth form level.

"to demonstrate the styles of librarians and teachers as managers of knowledge."

The picture being created is a detailed and comprehensive view of actual behaviour, events, attitudes and problems. The project archives will provide an authoritative bank of information about how things really are, not how we think they are -- or would like them to be.

Research is also examining student learning styles in secondary schools,[18] a neglected area for librarians and many teachers. Students may have preferred learning styles which condition the way in which they gather, process and use information. If we can discern these different styles and match them more closely with the preferred styles of teachers, then the resulting interaction should be more efficient. Whether or not librarians attempt to teach teachers or users, such information is essential to the process of communication of whatever knowledge and skills are considered appropriate.

The same research is also considering assignments, and the demands they make upon students and styles. We know little about *how* students approach their work -- the 'information skills curriculum' mentioned earlier is but one synthesis of what seems to happen. Hence an investigation has begun[19] which will probe the expectations of teachers and students, monitor students' decisions upon attempting their learning tasks, their planned and actual actions and assessments of students' completed tasks as compared with teachers' expectations.

Elsewhere,[20] the study skills of students in further education are being examined within the context of demands imposed by institutional policy, subject disciplines, textbooks, work assignments, and time. All forms of user education offer risks to students; at the time of instruction students may not perceive direct benefits and additional work may seem irrelevant. Only by examining the context within which an individual student studies can we appreciate the nature and complexity of such risks, and whether or not improved information skills are an appropriate goal for students under pressure.

Moving to the more specific tasks associated with text-interrogation, the 'Reading for Learning in the Secondary School' project[21] has concentrated on the development of teaching materials to help teachers prepare students for tackling printed material, especially school textbooks. Earlier work by the team[22] provided insights into the nature and problems of a wide range of reading-related tasks in schools, including some gems on student use of libraries.

Links to Learning in Higher Education

Much of the work described in this paper has centered upon practice and research in secondary schools but the links with the tertiary sector are strong. That there is so much activity in secondary schools is partly the product of tertiary and higher education institutions' concern for *their* student difficulties and deficiencies. The British Library Research and Development Department's interests and support have followed a similar path. Universitites, polytechnics and colleges have been engaged in user education for many years and librarians have often described their work as remedial.

The curious development from the shift to school level work has been the creation of a new lead. Much the same could be said of school level work in the U.S.A. But whilst we are leading in terms of closer connections between librarians, teachers and students, and are, therefore, working on similar problems for similar reasons, we have rejected one particular phenomenon which exists in other sectors. Evaluation of information of study skills programmes has not become a major issue in British schools. It is an interesting departure or divergence which may best be explained by reference to the wealth of evaluation techniques which have certainly measured what *has been* taught to library users, but not what *should* have been taught — whatever that may mean! We cannot, in the long term, measure information skills as applied to information use because students pass through our libraries and into society. It is only when they exercise fair and reasonable judgement, based on rational thought and informed decision-making that we can really assess their ability to use information. If, in the future, school library users *do* know how to "look for the circumstances they want" and make them if none is found, then we can evaluate our education and training. If using libraries is 'good' for students we should be evaluating the 'goodness' rather than whether or not they can find the height of the Tower of London in a reference book.

British librarians and teachers now have a forum for the discussion of user education in schools, funded by the British Library Research and Development Department and attended by representatives from most of the projects mentioned in this paper. Its links with further and higher education are clear and strong, and we think the prospects for moving forward are good because the discussion group not only shares information about current activities but also plans future work.

Perhaps we will discover what is meant by the term 'goodness' and why it is that using libraries and information is 'good' for students. We will certainly try. For this is what competence is all about.

'When *I* use a word,' Humpty Dumpty said, in a rather scornful tone, 'it means just what I choose it to mean — neither more nor less.' 'The question is,' said Alice, 'whether you *can* make words mean so many different things.' 'The question is,' said Humpty Dumpty, 'which is to be master — that's all.'

Lewis Carroll: Through the Looking Glass

NOTES

1. Nordling, Jo Anne. "The High School Library and the Classroom: Closing the Gap." In Lubans, J. ed. *Progress in Educating the Library User*. Bowker, 1978, pp. 45–55.

2. Lubans, John. "Evaluating Library-User Education Programmes." *Drexel Library Quarterly*, 8(3), 1972, pp. 325–343.

3. Bibliographies covering the period include:
Malley, Ian, compiler. *Education in the Use of Libraries and Information — A Bibliography*. Part 1, pre 1900–1954; Part 2, 1955–1969; Part 3, 1970–1975; Part 4, 1976–1979. British

Library Information Officer for User Education, Loughborough University, 1980– .

Lockwood, Deborah, compiler. *Library Instruction: A Bibliography*. Greenwood Press, 1979.

Taylor, Peter; Harris, Colin; Clark, Daphne, compilers. *The Education of Users of Library and Information Services: An International Bibliography, 1926–1976*. London: Aslib, 1979.

4. Henne, Frances. "Learning to Learn in School Libraries." *School Libraries*, 15(4), 1966, pp. 15;23.

5. Brittain, J. Michael. *Instruction of Students in the Handling of Information*. Paper presented to the NATO Information Science Advanced Study Institute, College of Librarianship Wales, August 1973.

6. *Information Skills in the Secondary Curriculum*, edited by Michael Marland. Schools Council Curriculum Bulletin 9. Methuen Educational, 1981.

7. Brake, Terence. "Information Skills in Context: An Account of the Information Skills in the Curriculum Research Unit." In Malley, Ian, editor. *Current R & D Projects in User Education in the U.K., 1980*. British Library Information Officer for User Education, Loughborough University, 1980.

8. Gibbs, Graham. *Learning to Study: A Guide to Running Group Sessions*. Institute of Educational Technology, Tuition and Counselling Research Group, The Open University, 1977.

9. Tabberer, Ralph and Allman, Janet. *Study Skills at 16 Plus* (Research in Progress 4) National Foundation for Educational Research, 1981.

10. Buzan, Tony. *Use Your Head*. BBC Publications, 1974.

11. de Bono, Edward. *Teaching Thinking*. Maurice Temple Smith, 1976.

12. Brake, Terence. *The Need to Know: Teaching the Importance of Information*. (British Library Research and Development Report 5511) British Library, 1980.

13. Brake, Terence. *User Education Is Dead. Long Live Education.*

Paper presented to the Second International Conference on User Education, Keble College, Oxford, 1981. (To be published by the British Library.)

14. Lubans, John. "Introduction: Seeking a Partnership Between the Teacher and the Librarian." In *Progress in Educating the Library User*. Bowker, 1978.

15. Perkins, Ralph. *The Prospective Teacher's Knowledge of Library Fundamentals*. Scarecrow Press, 1965.

    Hounsell, Dai, and others. *Educational Information and the Teacher*. (British Library Research and Development Report 5505.) British Library, 1980.

16. House of Commons. Education, Science and Arts Committee. *Fourth Report: Information Storage and Retrieval in the British Library Service* (House of Commons Paper 767--409 I to IV). HMSO, 1980.

17. Labbett, Beverley. "Library Access and Sixth Form Studies." Ian Malley, Ian, editor, *Current R & D Projects in User Education in the U.K., 1981*. British Library Information Officer for User Education, Loughborough University, 1981.

18. Martin, Elaine. "Information Use and Learning Style." In Malley, Ian, editor, *Current R & D Projects in User Education in the U.K., 1981*. British Library Information Officer for User Education, Loughborough University, 1981.

19. Stannett, Annette. *Student Decision-Making.* Institute for Educational Technology, University of Surrey, 1980-- .

20. Swatridge, Colin. *The Study Skills and Habits of Students on Advanced-Level Courses, with Particular Reference to Their Capacity for Independent Work*. School of Education, Nottingham University, 1980-- .

21. Lunzer, Eric A. and Keith Gardner. *Reading for Learning in the Secondary School*. School of Education, Nottingham University, 1978-- .

22. Lunzer, Eric A. and Keith Gardner, editors. *The Effective Use of Reading*. Heinemann Educational Books, for the Schools Council, 1979.

THE OHIO SCHOOL LIBRARY MEDIA TEST

Anne Hyland
Northeastern Ohio (Springfield) Local School District

We believe that libraries make a difference, that they benefit the educational process, specifically student achievement. We *BE-LIEVE* that, but this is an age of accountability. The bill payers want to know specifically what difference does it make in the education students receive that there are libraries and librarians available for students. "Document the difference to me," they say. "People are better, more whole, better able to cope," we say. "It's my money. Show me," they say. I feel very responsible for the proper expense of other people's money.

As a profession we have tried to supply that documentation over the years. We have done a number of studies to see if libraries and librarians made a difference. As I looked at the studies, they fell into four categories. These examined the increasing degree of involvement between the library program and the user's achievement. At the first level, they looked at the mere availability of libraries. This seems to me to be much like putting a chemistry lab in a school, letting students walk by it and hope that they learn all about chemistry. The next level of involvement was student use of available libraries. Next was student instruction in the use of available libraries. And finally, the studies looked at the student's ability to use the library. This last area is the one I was interested in. Student ability should be the variable under study. In those studies, locally developed tests had been used. They had developed the tests to fit their programs. They were not generalizable to other locations. I needed a test. I needed to document the difference libraries made in a student's ability. I really want to correlate that ability with other achievement, but first things first.

When we set up a program, any program, we ask ourselves, "What are my expectations? How will students be different when we're through?" These become the goals and objectives. They tell us where we are going so that we are more likely to get there. These goals and objectives are observable in some way. Some are paper and pencil measureable; not all are. If changes are observable, they can be documented, changes noted. This makes us focus our expectations on what we want to happen. We can be more deliberate and more systematic in what we do.

In order to set the development of the Ohio School Library Media Test into perspective I need to describe some of the beliefs I have about the public schools.

1. Our students are a very specific and well-defined group. They stay with us for 13 years. We have a long time to work with them. The parents stay around for a long time so that their expectations of what a public school ought to do, do not change rapidly. Also, students progress through the scope and sequence of instruction in a rather systematic and orderly fashion. The notion of continuous progress toward a predetermined end is explicit.

In terms of library instruction, it appears that the expectations for students are basically the same. But we do expect that students should become better at using the skills. This clearly points to the need for a K–12 continuous look at everything we do. It also makes us take notice of how the information comes to the student. How do students process information?

2. K--12 education is designed to be a *general* education. No one majors in fourth grade. Adults will never again pick up their Houghton--Mifflin text to learn the latest social studies concepts. The K--12 program is clearly a process of preparation for later living in other environments. In the library program our challenge is to focus, then, upon the most transferable concepts. We cannot spend of lot of time dealing with how to use a very specific tool, but rather must focus on the basic concept construction of the tool – the general formats which are transferable. There is a list provided by Mary George in your packets. They are things like: libraries use symbols – symbols are explained. Most information is indexed. There is order in the way information is arranged.

3. School library media centers exist within an educational institution with rather specific expectations. The library is only one part of that program and must be responsive to it. We can and ought to do a better job of what we uniquely can do. Students should be able to use well the resources we do have which are useful to them. And they ought to be able to transfer the basic concepts which are transferable library to library. Unfortunately there are fewer and fewer constants. We work with the card catalog for example and then the student winds up in a college or public library with all the information on a data base. We work with the *Readers' Guide* and they move on to a college where they need to use the *New York*

Times Index. The formats are very different. We spend a great deal of time with the development of an interest in reading for pleasure. Where is the casual reading in a college library? We spend time working with the Dewey System which facilitates browsing, and they find themselves with any number of other systems. Have you ever tried to browse children's literature collections in an LC set up? It is impossible. Librarians are the ones who throw stumbling blocks in the way of students trying to get their hands on information.

4. "Begin where the students are," is an old saying, but it is true. Sometimes the "students" we need to be working with are the teachers. They are just as important to the school process and the school library's effectiveness as are the students. It upsets me that a brand new teacher, fresh out of college, does not know how to keep up with the subject area he or she has been trained in. But, if that is the way teachers come to me, then I need to train them too.

5. One more perspective I have about public schools and the library programs in them is that I am not the little league for librarianship. I am not supposed to be training students to be self contained librarians. I am training them to be able to find the information they need, when they need it, in a way that is no more detailed or complicated than they need. Students will always travel the fastest route between two points. And if the card catalog is not needed, they will not use it.

Keeping all of that in mind, several years ago I needed a test in order to work with a group of sixth grade students. I found mention of some 31 tests, including nine which were subtests of general achievement tests. They were old, and dealt only with print materials. There was no statistical information on the great majority of them, many were out of print, and they had doubtful reliability. More importantly, I felt that the tests viewed library skills in terms of classes of information sources, rather than approaching the area from the thought processes students must use in order to be successful media center users.

The procedures used to develop the test were divided into several steps. I consider the development of the Table of Specifications critical to the whole process, because it makes the test very responsive to what we say we are teaching. The Table of Specifications is a list of skills which are to be tested, our goals and expectations. To develop this I examined elementary, secondary, and college library curriculum guides from all over the country. There are many many fine examples available. The ALA headquarters library has a good collection. I used the AASL/AECT national standards, the North

Central Association standards and our Ohio state standards. And I used the professional writing of noted experts in the field. I tallied the skills these sources indicated were important. A list of 27 skills in five broad areas emerged. The test questions were developed for these skills in the same ratios as indicated on the tallies.

Other tests available were matched to these areas. The tests correlate well with each other but do not match with what we say we do. (Tables 1 and 2.)

The five skills groupings view the library learning process from the student's perspective. They are presented here and on the test in logical thought process order according to Bloom's cognitive taxonomy. I also assumed in the test construction that non-print items were as important as print items for information gathering for students, and this emphasis is reflected in the questions.

In Table 3 *organization* refers to the basic floor plan and workings of the school media center space. Once the student has arrived in a specific location, *selection* skills are needed to choose the most appropriate resources. *Utilization* skills are needed to effectively use each type of material. *Comprehension* skills are those needed to gain meaning from resources. And, finally, any time a student is asked to take information from one source, translate it through personal experiences, and give it back to someone else, it is a *production*. The student's mind must sift through everything learned, select the necessary details and communicate a thought to someone.

Test items were written in accordance with several specific criteria. Next, the test was piloted using a panel of 83 experts and 135 students, and some statistics. The questions were revised according to these findings, and the final instrument was administered to 2,670 students in grades 4–12 in May, 1978. More statistics followed. We had added in, by the way, possible variables such as wealth of the district, money spent per pupil, and availability of professional media persons, aides, and/or volunteers.

We were very pleased with the final results. We had set levels for statistical expectations and these were met or exceeded. The test has an internal consistency coefficient of .899. This is the degree to which the items measure the same variable. Anything above .7 would have been acceptable. We also established grade level norms on those 2,670 students who took the test.

There are weak questions on the test, and I would probably change them if it were to be revised. But that would be very costly to re-validate the test, and the internal consistency would not become much greater.

The test is strong and valid. It can be used to measure a student's library media ability. I have had more demand for it than I can keep up with, which tells me that there is an enormous need for some type of sound, valid measurement instrument.

Carolyn asked me to mention why I think the test is better than the others. I'm not sure that "better" is an appropriate word, different than the others might be more to the point. I am confident that this Table of Specifications is fairly accurate, and that ought to make us relook at what we are teaching, and therefore testing. I am pleased that this test at least makes an attempt to look at the higher levels of skills students need. The last two areas, Comprehension and Production, are the ones which will be most transferable library to library, and yet they receive only about 30% of the emphasis in instructional programs. The first two areas, Organization and Selection are often drastically different from library to library. The Utilization section items are generally applicable library to library. A periodical guide will have a different title and index different materials, but it works the same once you get into it.

I am pleased with the solid statistics of the test. The statistician who worked on this did not care at all about the content. He wanted to make certain that it was defensible. I am very glad he was aware of the importance of reliable instruments.

I am pleased that the test can be scored by learning objective, and therefore directs future instruction to points where it will be needed. And I am pleased that the questions are trying to present informational thought processes needed to ask or answer real concerns. The questions are not meant to be tricky, technical questions.

I am also pleased that the test addresses the need which K--12 programs have for their instruction. They are not training future librarians, they must focus on processes and techniques, and they must work with all other teachers in order to do that instruction well. This test is looking at ways students process information.

I think it also makes us look at *our* instructional programs and examine our professional approach to library skill instruction. Does it work with the curriculum from beginning to end? Or does it stand as another subject for students to learn in an isolated way? What difference does it make to the education of students that we are there?

TABLE 1

Library Media Skill Areas Measured on Subtests of
General Achievement Tests

SKILLS	Iowa	Iowa Every Pupil	CTB (2 levels)	McGraw	Spitzer	Stanford
Organization						
library citizenship						
acquaint with other information agencies in the community						
organization of the library			X			
Dewey Decimal						
Dewey arrangement		X				
alphabetical order				X		
Selection						
kinds of media available for use						
parts of the catalog card				X		
use of the card catalog						
choosing type and level of materials						
periodical guides						
abbreviations						
Utilization						
use of reference books	X	X	X	X	X	
use of parts of books		X	X	X	X	
government documents						
use of equipment						
gather information from sources other than libraries						
Comprehension						
self direction in reading						
reading skills						
listening and viewing skills	X					
study and work skills				X	X	
research process						
classify information						
synthesizing						
sound judgment in use of newspapers, periodicals, and indexes						
maps and graphs	X	X	X		X	
Production						
bibliographic form						
speaking and writing to communicate						
production of graphics and other media						

(Stanford: out-of-print, not available for review)

TABLE 2

Library Media Skill Areas Measured on Accessible Library Tests

SKILLS	Bennett 1947	Feagley 1961	Gullette 1967, 74	Perfection I 1967	Perfection II 1967	Perfection III 1967	Stephensen 1960	Peabody 1938, 40	Smith 1940	Tyler-Kimber 1937	Nationwide 1962	Ploeg 1942
Organization												
library citizenship												
acquaint with other information agencies												
organization of the library	X	X	X	X						X	X	
Dewey Decimal	X		X	X	X	X	X				X	
Dewey arrangement			X						X			X
alphabetical order	X		X		X	X					X	
Selection												
kinds of media available for use												
parts of catalog card	X	X	X								X	
use of card catalog	X	X	X			X	X	X	X	X	X	X
choosing type and level of materials								X				
periodical guides	X	X	X	X	X	X	X	X		X	X	X
abbreviations		X								X	X	X
Utilization												
use of reference books	X	X	X	X	X	X	X	X		X	X	X
use of parts of books	X		X	X	X		X	X	X	X	X	X
government documents												
use of equipment												
gather information from sources other than libraries												
Comprehension												
self direction in reading												
reading skills												
listening and viewing												
study and work skills	X				X							
research process												
classify information												
synthesizing												
sound judgment in use of newspapers, periodicals, and indexes												
maps and graphs			X							X		
Production												
bibliographic form							X	X				
speaking and writing to communicate				X								
production of graphics and other media												

TABLE 2
(continued)

Descriptive Information

	Bennett 1947	Feagley 1961	Gullette 1967, 74	Perfection I 1967	Perfection II 1967	Perfection III 1967	Stephensen 1960	Peabody 1938, 40	Smith 1940	Tyler-Kimber 1937	Nationwide 1962	Ploeg 1942
Out-of-print	Y	?	Y'67 N'74	?	?	?	Y	Y	Y	Y	N	Y
Reviewed	Y	Y	Y'67 N'74	L	L	L	Y	Y	Y	Y	L	Y
Norms provided	N	Y	N	N	N	N	N	N	N	?	Y	Y
Validity information provided	?	Y	N	N	N	N	N	Y	N	?	N	Y
Reliability information provided	Y	Y	N	N	N	N	N	Y	?	?	N	N

Y = Yes
N = No
L = Listed only
? = Information available is unclear

TABLE 3

BASIC LIBRARY INSTRUCTION SKILL GROUPINGS

ORGANIZATION

    Library citizenship
    Acquaintance with other information agencies in the community
    Organization of the library
    Dewey Decimal system
    Dewey arrangement
    Alphabetical order

SELECTION

    Kinds of media available for use
    Parts of the catalog card
    Use of the card catalog
    Choice of type and level of materials
    Selection from periodical guides
    Selecting appropriate information sources for the task

UTILIZATION

    Use of reference books
    Use of parts of books
    Use of government documents
    Use of equipment
    Using sources other than libraries for information

COMPREHENSION

    Self-direction in reading: literature appreciation
    Reading skills
    Listening and viewing skills; including film/media appreciation
    Study skills: note taking, outlining, follow directions, use of
        bibliographies to locate information
    Research skills: paraphrase information, narrow or broaden a
        topic, selecting a problem, synthesizing information, critical
        judgments in use of information sources

PRODUCTION

    Develop bibliographies
    Speaking and writing to communicate
    Production of graphics and other media
    Evaluation of communication products

MANUAL FOR

OHIO SCHOOL LIBRARY/MEDIA TEST

CONTENTS

DEVELOPMENT OF TEST

Overview. For one hundred and fifty years it has been assumed that students who have access to school library facilities will learn to use those facilities in such a way as to increase their academic success. A dozen research studies have attempted to establish such a relationship, but have been limited by the lack of a suitable measurement instrument. Library skills tests which have been developed over the years are not adequate for current use because they (a) are out-of-print, (b) are not statistically supported, of (c) do not measure all skill areas.

This study, therefore, developed an instrument which could be used to measure school library/media ability in fourth through twelfth grade students. In order to insure a reliable test the developer was concerned with assuring content validity, and construct validity in the form of group differences, item analysis and internal consistency.

Methodology. The study was divided into two phases. The first phase was concerned with establishing the content validity of the test. Content validity is the systematic examination of the test content to determine whether it covers a representative sample of the behavior to be measured.

During this first phase a table of specifications was developed by consulting a collection of about 60 national and state elementary, secondary, and college curriculum guides in the field of school library/media skills; national, regional, and state standards; and professional judgements. All possible skills cited were noted and tallied. Total tallies for each category were adjusted to percentages of the total category so that each would carry equal weight in the final analysis. Pilot instrument items were written in the same quantity and for the same skills as those identified in the table of specifications. The skills fell logically into five broad areas: Organization, Selection, Utilization, Comprehension, and Production. These were arranged on the test in hierarchical order from skills requiring least cognitive ability to those requiring the most ability.

Content Validity of the instrument was also assessed by a panel of 68 persons. These were persons who were officers or chairpersons of the Ohio professional school library media association, and persons whom the association has identified to assist with regional accreditation inspections. The pilot instrument was also administered to 135 students. A difficulty index, a discrimination index, a coefficient of internal consistency and a correlation coefficient were obtained from the pilot testing.

The second phase began by analyzing and rewriting test items according to the statistical information obtained in the pilot testing, and according to the comments and concerns of the panel of experts. (Table 1 identifies the relationship between questions developed and specific skills). The second phase was also concerned with establishing acceptable levels of construct validity. Construct validity is an analysis of the meaning of test scores in terms of psychological concepts. In this study evidence supporting the construct validity was measured in the pilot study by comparing scores of students with previous library media training against scores of students without previous training. Evidence supporting the construct validity on the final testing was measured by comparing various student and school district factors against student scores and by item analysis and internal consistency.

Group Differences. The school and student factors were designed to identify group differences as well as account for possible external factors. These factors were: availability of a library media center, availability of full or part-time library media professionals, availability of full or part-time aides or volunteers, the relative wealth of a school district, and the relative wealth of the school system. Analysis of Variance techniques were used to determine what effect each had upon student scores.

Item Analysis. A discrimination index and a difficulty index were obtained for each item on the final instrument Discrimination index scores of .3 or greater would indicate a moderate to high correlation with a person's overall test score. Difficulty index scores between .3 and .7 would indicate test questions in the middle range of difficulty.

Internal Consistency. Internal consistency is an indication that the test items measure the same variable. The expectation was that the test items in the **Ohio School Library Media Test** would correlate with the total test at a technically acceptable level of .7 or above. Such evidence would serve to support the internal consistency of the instrument. The statistical procedure used to test this expectation was the Kuder-Richardson 20 Formula.

RELIABILITY

Construct Validity—Group Differences. Student scores were analyzed according to five groups: sex, grade, relative cost per pupil, relative wealth per pupil, and type of library assistance available to students. Differences between logical groups would lend construct support to the final instrument. **Sex.** In the final analysis females scored higher than males. This is in keeping with research findings in the field of sex differences. **Grade Level.** Higher grade levels scored highest on the test. This is in keeping with the basic assumption of the test, that skills are learned and perfected through time and practice. **Cost Per Pupil.** Student from districts which spent most per pupil for education scored highest. This supports generally held assumptions of school finance. **Wealth Per Pupil.** Students from the least wealthy and the most wealthy districts scored highest. Taking into consideration Ohio school finance structure, the wealth of the district was not as important as the community's desire to provide a quality education for their students. This finding supported that notion. **Available Assistance.** All combinations which included a full time professional scored higher than any combination with a part-time professional. It is logical to expect that full time assistance will be more effective than part time assistance. These findings supported the construct validity of the test.

Construct Validity—Item Analysis. A discrimination index of .3 or greater and a difficulty index between .3 and .7 would lend construct support to the final instrument. Eight of the questions have discrimination index scores below

.3, all others were greater than .3. Difficulty index scores for grades 4-9 and for combined grades were between .3 and .7. Scores for grades 10-12 were only slightly above .7. The reported scores generally support the construct validity of the final instrument.

Construct Validity—Internal Cosistency. A technically acceptable level of .7 or above was expected for the K-R 20 correlation and would indicate a high degree of homogeneity. The correlations are the strongest (.85 to .89) for the total test (53 questions). Individual subsections correlate less well (.47 to .72). In each case the Production subsection correlation is the weakest (.35 to .52). The correlations indicate that the total test is the best predictor of a student's library/media ability.

A Varimax rotated factor analysis was also obtained on the test items. It identified clusters of items which had some relationship to each other. Thirty-four (64%) of the 53 items were identified on the analysis. The eleven factors identified did cluster as expected, although not all items clustered.

NORMS AND SCALES

Grade Level Norms. The norms from the final testing are a level of achievement of the student population who took the test. Students with similar characteristics could be expected to perform on the test in a similar manner. The grade level norms and standard deviations from the final testing are provided in Table 2.

The student sample was 2670 students. The test was administered in May of 1978. The students represented 33 school districts from across Ohio, and represented an equitable distribution from rural, suburban and urban settings.

AIDS TO INTERPRETATION OF SCORES

Content Domain. The test is based on several assumptions. **One**: That school library/media skills stay constant, but students become better and better users as they practice the skills in realistic situations. **Two**: nonprint items are as important as print forms for information gathering. **Three**: Previous library tests viewed library skills in terms of classes of information sources, rather than approaching the area from the thought processes students must use in order to be successful media center users. **Four**: If you were to read the questions for previous library tests and imagine the type of setting they were describing you would picture a totally print world. This image does not match with today's school library media center.

The five broad areas identified in the test are arranged in logical thought process order. The **first** section is Organization—as a student enters the media center space, what needs to be known about how things are organized in order to find what is needed? **Second**: Selection—once a student is familiar with how things are arranged, what skills are needed in order to select appropriate resources? **Third**: Utilization—once a student has selected several resources, what skills are needed in order to make proper use of the resource (this includes print and nonprint resources). **Fourth**: Comprehension—once the skills for locating the appropriate parts of a resource are used, what skills does a student need in order to understand the given information? **Fifth**: production—once the student understands the concepts and ideas available, what skills are needed by the student to present that information in a meaningful way back to others? Writing reports are included in this last section, along with other ways students share what they have learned with others.

Test applications. The test can be used to identify specific skills students need further instruction in; or it can identify one or more specific subsections where students need additional instruction; or the overall test score can provide an indication of a students general library media ability. This score can also be compared to the norm sample to compare one group of students to the sample group of students.

ADMINISTRATION AND SCORING

The test is designed to be taken by students in grades 4 through 12. Students should have an uncluttered and cleared area. They will each need a pencil, a test booklet, and an answer sheet.

The instructions on page one should be reviewed with the students. These instructions are based on the use of a computer readable answer sheet. You may use any type of answer sheet however. Do be certain that each student understands how they are to mark the correct answer on the answer sheet. Also check to be certain that each student has their name and any other information you may wish to have on the top of the answer sheets.

STRESS THAT STUDENTS ARE NOT TO MARK IN THE TEST BOOKLET.

After you are satisfied that each student knows how to mark their answer on the answer sheet, the students may begin. The test is not timed. Students should be instructed to do the best they can. Guessing should be permitted.

When students ask for assistance with vocabulary or other phrases, DO NOT ANSWER THEIR QUESTIONS. Tell them to do the best they can. (I have found that they ask those questions of the teacher when that word or phrase is what is being tested!).

Scoring. Correct answers are provided in this manual. Mark those which students have answered wrong. Do not count question 44. This will give each student one additional point.

You can examine the scores either by the five subsections, or for the total test, or by individual skills (which are noted in Table 1). You will then be able to pin point the most effective place to focus your instruction. If you score the whole test and are considering only the total test score, you can compare your student scores to the Ohio norm sample found in Table 2.

SUGGESTIONS FOR USE

1.   The test can be used to identify areas where students do or do not need additional library instruction.

2.   The test can be used as a pre-test/posttest to determine the effectiveness of library instruction.

3.   The test can be used to verify areas of need when applying for grants or specialized funding.

4.   The test can be used for correlation studies between library/media skills and general academic achievement or with specific subject area achievement.

5.   The test can be used to determine if special funding such as Title I or impacted funds has an effect on student skills.

6.   The test can be used to identify general trends in student library/media ability.

7.   The test can be used with various library instructional techniques to determine which is most effective.

8.   At the district level the test can be used to correlate unique building or area factors to determine which ones most effect achievement.

TABLE 1

SKILL AREAS OF OHIO SCHOOL LIBRARY MEDIA TEST

Skills	Item Number
Organization	
library citizenship	1
other information agencies	-
organization of library	2, 3, 4
Dewey Decimal	5, 6
Dewey arrangement	7, 8
alphabetical order	9, 10
Selection	
kinds of media available for use	11, 12
parts of catalog card	13, 14, 15
use of card catalog	16, 17
choosing type and level of materials	18, 19, 20, 21
periodical guides	22, 23, 24, 25
Utilization	
use of reference books	27, 28
use of parts of books	29, 30, 31, 32
government documents	26
use of equipment	33, 34, 35, 36
use of other sources	-
Comprehension	
self direction in reading	-
reading skills	37, 38
listening and viewing	42, 43
study and work skills	39, 40, 41, 44
research process	
classify information	
synthesizing	
judgement in use of newspapers, periodicals	
and indexes	45, 46
Production	
bibliographic form	52, 53
speaking and writing to communicate	51
production of graphics and other media	47, 48, 49, 50

-6-

TABLE 2

**Mean Scores and Standard Deviation of Final Instrument

Grade	No. of Students	Organization	Selection	Utilization	Comprehension	Production	Total
4-6	946	5.607	8.086	5.874	4.741	3.258	27.566**
sd		2.2	2.8	2.3	1.9	1.6	8.5
7-9	832	6.513	9.834	7.014	5.624	3.745	32.731**
sd		1.9	2.5	2.2	2.2	1.6	8.2
10-12	884	7.624	11.216	8.269	7.035	4.869	39.014**
sd		1.7	2.5	2.1	2.1	1.8	8.2

These are the mean scores of the sample of 2670 students. Use these scores to compare your students to this group of students.

** A Mean score is the "norm" average for the group of students who took the test. If your students are similar to these students, your students should score in a comparable range to these students. If your students are different, their scores will be different. The differences could be attributed to many factors. This test provides strong indications that the differences can, possibly, be attributed to the student's school library media ability.

OHIO SCHOOL LIBRARY/MEDIA TEST
correct answers

Organization			Utilization	
1	B		*26	B
2	C		27	B
3	C		28	A
4	A		29	C
5	B		30	A
*6	C		31	D
7	B		32	B
8	A		33	A
9	A		34	B
10	C		35	D
			36	B

Selection			Comprehension	
11	C		37	B
12	A		38	C
*13	B		*39	C
14	B		40	C
15	C		41	D
16	A		42	B
17	D		43	D
18	C		*44	A
19	B		45	B
20	D		46	D
21	C			
22	C		Production	
23	B			
24	D		47	D
25	B		48	C
			49	A
			50	D
			51	B
			52	C
			53	B

* Items with low correlations, meaning that the answers students selected for these items do not correlate well with the other answers they selected. I judge that students do not know 6, 13, 26. They have not done enough search strategy thinking to answer 39. Question 44 is not well written. It is really the only one on the test which should be disgarded. When scoring simply ignore, thereby adding 1 to each total score.

PROFILE OF LIBRARY SKILLS IN OHIO[1]

Anne Hyland

Problem

We have a theory in the school media profession that media centers in schools benefit the educational process — specifically student achievement. Several years ago I wanted to work with a group of energetic teachers and gather some additional evidence for this theory. But I needed to be able to test student library/media achievement. I needed to know how much students already knew before we began our study and I wanted to be able to see if there had been an increase in achievement after the study. I also wanted to know what specific skills students were weakest in so that I could focus instruction on areas of need.

So, I tried to locate a suitable test for a group of regular, normal everyday 6th grade students. No Such Luck. I found mention of some 31 including 9 which were subtests of general achievement tests. Only one had a copyright date after 1970 and it was a reprinting of an earlier test. All were very dated — all dealt with only print materials. There was no statistical information available, they had doubtful reliability, and maybe more importantly, I felt that the tests viewed library skills in terms of classes of information sources, rather than approaching the area from the thought processes students must use in order to be successful media center users. None of the tests had good, strong, positive reviews!

Well, what next? What had people done before when faced with this same problem? I gathered a dozen studies which had tried to examine the relationship between school media programs and any kind of student acheivement. In the cases where student library ability HAD been tested the researchers had developed local instruments for their study. They had not tried to create a statistically sound instrument. As a result their studies were not very generalizable. I did not feel I could use the tests available.

from: **Ohio Media Spectrum**, Vol. 31, No. 4, Winter 1979. Pages 12-17.

[1] This article is based on a presentation made by Anne Hyland at the ALA national convention in Dallas Texas on June 24, 1979 at the AASL Research Forum.

Solution – Construct a Test

Necessity being the mother of invention – I set about to develop an instrument which could be used to measure school library/media ability in 4th through 12th grade students. (Fourth grade is used as the bottom range because of the varied reading level of students below this age.)

The procedures used to develop the test were divided into several steps. I consider the development of the Table of Specifications critical to the whole process because it makes this test very responsive to what we say we are teaching – in contrast to the other tests available which correlate well with each other but not with what we say we do. The Table of Specifications is the list of skills which would be tested. I examined elementary, secondary, and college library curriculum guides from all over the country. I used AASL/AECT national standards, North Central Association standards, and Ohio Department of Education standards; and I used the professional writing of experts in the field. I tallied the skills these sources indicated were important. A list of 27 skills in 5 broad areas emerged. (Table 1) The test questions were developed for these areas and skills in the same ratios as indicated on the tallies.

I arranged the 5 broad areas in logical thought process order. The first section is *Organization* – as a student enters the media center space, what needs to be known about how things are organized? The second section is *Selection* – once a student is familiar with how things are arranged, what skills are needed to select appropriate resources? The third section is *Utilization* – once a student has selected several resources, what skills are needed in order to make proper use of each print or non-print resource? The fourth section is *Comprehension* – once the skills for locating the appropriate parts of a resource are used, what skills does a student need in order to understand the information given? The fifth section is *Production* – once the student understands the concepts and ideas available, what skills are needed by the student to present that information in a meaningful way back to others? Writing reports are included in this section along with other ways students share what they have learned with others.

For anyone interested in doing their own test construction this next step is most important . . . find lots of friends who are willing to help! I ask Ohio media persons for help and they were overwhelmingly willing to assist. It was very encouraging. It also explains why media programs are as strong as they are – we work with very dedicated, very capable people. Programs are strong because of the people in them.

Next, we did a pilot testing of the first set of test items (the pilot instrument) using a panel of 83 experts, 135 students, and some statistical analysis. The questions were revised according to these findings and the final instrument was administered to 2670 Ohio students in grades 4-12 in May of 1978.

More statistics followed. We had added in, by the way, possible variables such as wealth of the district, money spent per student, and availability of professional media persons, aides, and/or volunteers.

We were very pleased with the results of the final analysis. We had set levels for statistical expectations and these were met or exceeded. We had an internal consistency coefficient of .899 (anything above .7 would have been acceptable.) That .899 is the degree to which the items measure the same variable. We also established grade level norms based on the 2670 students who took the test. These norms are provided in Table 2.

In question by question analysis there is really only one question which contributes nothing to a student's total test score information. Of the 5 subsections the Production one is the weakest and probably won't give you much useful information about a student's ability if used by itself. The others will.

The test is strong and valid. You can use it to measure a student's libra y media ability. I have used it with a different group of 6th grade students and I was able to analyze specific weak areas and group students for instruction in those areas. The test could be used to verify a student need when applying for special project money, and could be used in a posttest situation to show the results of some type of treatment. The test could be used to see if students who score high in library/media center ability are also high scorers on other achievement tests. The test is called the *Ohio School Library/Media Test* and has 53 questions in 5 skills areas.

On the Way to Constructing a Test

I have some other bits of information which are not related to construction or validation of the test; but are very interesting and turned up on the way to constructing the test. We used the answers from the 2670 students to establish the statistical base. However, it also gave us a good idea about what skills students have or have not mastered. One of the assumptions of the test construction was that student skill increases over time. That is, as students get older they learn more, practice more, and score better on this test. So, by examining the response percentages for the grade levels we can tell if increases had or had not taken place as expected.

Increases – this they learned

There are 7 areas where knowledge had increased:

1) Students learn most of the library terms, such as fiction, nonfiction and periodical (Biography is still fuzzy for most however.)

2) The greatest increases of all those reported were for placing Dewey numbers in proper order. By the upper grades this is learned!

3) Students learn well what types of resources media centers can provide.

4) Students learn well how to use reference books and encyclopedias, including table of contents and the index.

5) Students learn what type of media is appropriate for specific types of equipment.

6) Students are familiar with sections in newspapers.

7) Students get better at using context clues and illustrations when reading for meaning.

Small increases – this they have not learned

There were 5 areas where there was little if any increase in knowledge over time. Either we don't teach these areas — or they really are not needed by students — or students need more practice in these areas — or all of the above.

1) This was the least well learned of all. There was practically no change over time. Students did not know which Dewey classification sections were associated with which broad subject areas. I suspect students never need to know this — or we never really teach it — but it was included on almost EVERY guide or standard I consulted during the test construction process.

2) Students did not learn what types of catalog cards are available, they did not know what information was provided on the card, they did not learn how the card catalog could be used (and not used), and they did not learn *library* alphabetical order. Considering all the time these catalogs take to maintain, we ought to teach better, or re-examine our use of the card catalog as the index to "everything".

3) Students did not learn to use a periodical index and did not learn what information is needed to find a periodical article.

4) Students did not learn how to begin to approach a research topic. I wasn't surprised about this one, but I was disappointed. We certainly ought to do better in this area.

5) Students did not learn bibliographic form — again, no surprise.

Other Bits of "isn't — that -- interesting"

Something else I ran across on my way to this test. As I compiled the percentages for the tallies it was obvious that elementary and secondary people don't talk to each other much. Elementary guides put 51% of their total skills in the first 2 of the 5 subsections. This is to be expected — you'd want to get the basics down well in the elementary grades. On the other hand, secondary guides put 57% of their total skills in those same first 2 subsections. Surely this is an overemphasis for secondary students. Maybe they really are as bored as they say. There are also 4 times as many elementary guides as secondary guides available, and maybe 5 of the 85 were K-12 sequenced. That does not speak well about our total media program efforts.

When we looked at the extra variables we had considered we found that it doesn't matter how wealthy the district is. It is more important how much parents are willing to support the education system. It also appears that a full-time ANYONE is more effective than a part-time anyone. Further study needs to be done with this one. Many of the larger school districts in Ohio, and a few of the small ones, use part-time professionals in elementary buildings. If such a practice contributes slightly or not at all to students achievement, alternative methods need to be explored.

One more aside. All of the subtests of the general achievement tests included map and chart reading as a skill in the library or study skill subtest. Not a single library/media guide or standard included that as a skill.

So What

So, we now have a test. It has been used on a large sample of students in Ohio, and for the record, it has been used on a large scale in North Carolina. We

—12—

know in what skill areas students do best, and we know in what skill areas students do not do well. We need to examine those weak areas and, perhaps, make a concentrated effort to put special emphasis in those instructional areas — provide more practice, provide teachers with ways to provide more practice.

We probably need to look at ourselves too, and examine our professional approach to library/media skill instruction. Does it work with the curriculum — from the beginning to the end? Or does it stand as another subject for students to learn?

I am hopeful that the availability of the test will provide useful information about student library/media ability. I also hope it will be useful to guide appropriate instruction.

THE OHIO SCHOOL LIBRARY/MEDIA TEST

DIRECTIONS TO THE STUDENT

The purpose of this test is to help your teacher or media specialist understand what you know about how to use the library/media center. There will be some questions which will not be familiar to you. Do the best you can and go on to the next question.

The person giving this test will read the directions out loud. Please read along with him.

1. This is not a timed test. Read each item. If you do not understand a question, go on to the next question.

2. Following each question there are four possible answers. Read each question and decide which answer is correct.

3. Choose the answer which you think is correct and darken the circle on your answer sheet. Mark only one answer for each question.

4. Make a heavy pencil mark on your answer sheet. Erase clearly any answer you wish to change.

5. DO NOT MARK IN THIS TEST BOOKLET.

EXAMPLE QUESTION

Which of the following would
you probably find in the school
library/media center?

   A. a horse
   B. a paperback book
   C. a car
   D. a swimming pool

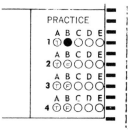

The correct answer is "a paperback book," which is lettered "B". If this question had been on the test you would have darkened the circle marked "B".

DO NOT TURN THIS PAGE UNTIL YOU ARE TOLD TO DO SO.

60

1. All the materials in the school media center are the property of the:

   A. librarian
   B. school
   C. principal
   D. teachers

2. In the school media center magazines are located in the:

   A. fiction area
   B. bibliography area
   C. periodical area
   D. audiovisual area

3. In the school media center materials about the real life of a real person are located in the:

   A. geography area
   B. fiction area
   C. biography area
   D. bibliography area

4. In the school media center a story that never really happened called *Snow Mountain*, written by *Herb Drummond* will be located in the:

   A. fiction section
   B. non-fiction section
   C. biography area
   D. Dewey Decimal numbered section

5. The Dewey Decimal system is used in school media centers because it:

   A. generally groups biographies with other fiction materials
   B. generally groups materials on the same subject together
   C. generally groups magazines with other audio-visual materials
   D. none of the above

6. In the school media center information about cars and airplanes will probably be in which general Dewey Decimal classification area?

   A. 200
   B. 400
   C. 600
   D. 800

Use this information to answer questions 7 and 8.

The following are Dewey Decimal classification numbers for different materials available in the school media center.

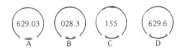

7. If the materials above were in proper order on a shelf, which would be the first one?

   A. 629.03
   B. 028.3
   C. 155
   D. 629.6

8. If the materials above were in proper order on a shelf, which would be the third one?

   A. 629.03
   B. 028.3
   C. 155
   D. 629.6

---

9. If the following titles were arranged in alphabetical order in the card catalog, which one would be the first?

   A. The First Dog Show
   B. Mexican Dances
   C. A Snowy Day
   D. An Ohio Landmark

10. If these authors were arranged in alphabetical order in the card catalog, which one would be the first?

    A. Cathy Apple
    B. Dianna Mattern
    C. Marilyn Alexander
    D. Janet Crandell

11. Which group of words lists a type of resource you would NOT find in a school media center?

A. films, filmstrips, transparencies
B. records, tapes, television
C. birth records, attendance reports
D. books, newspapers, magazines

12. Information about sea shells can be found by studying a:

A. filmstrip
B. globe
C. atlas
D. almanac

Use this catalog card to answer questions 13, 14 and 15.

```
                 The pirates
341.77           Poe, John Davis
                 The pirates; outlaws of the sea.
                 (Filmstrip)  Columbus, OH: SQA,
                 c1968.

                 filmstrip:32fr; col.




                              ◯
```

13. The catalog card above is:

A. an author card
B. a title card
C. a subject card
D. an analytic card

14. The catalog card above identifies a:

A. book
B. filmstrip
C. periodical
D. videotape

15. The catalog card above provides all the following information:

A. title, call number, pagination
B. author, title, editor
C. author, call number, copyright date
D. editor, place of publication, verso

—3—

16. The card catalog will give you location information for:

    A. a study print on snakes
    B. a magazine article on rockets
    C. an encyclopedia article on pottery
    D. baseball statistics in an almanac

17. If you know the title of a cassette tape you can use the card catalog to:

    A. find out where the tape is located in the media center
    B. find out who authored the tape
    C. see if the tape is checked out to someone
    D. A and B

18. Which of the following type of material could be used by a blind student?

    A. a picture book
    B. a captioned filmstrip
    C. a cassette tape
    D. a diazo transparency

19. Which of the following is the best source for finding a description of a famous person's life?

    A. *Information Please Almanac*
    B. *Current Biography*
    C. *Reader's Guide to Periodical Literature*
    D. *Guinness Book of World Records*

20. Which of the following will probably have **THE MOST** information on how to train birds to do many kinds of tricks?

    A. a magazine article
    B. a transparency
    C. an 8mm film loop
    D. a book

21. Which of the following will probably have the **MOST RECENT** information available on a topic?

    A. an encyclopedia
    B. a book
    C. a magazine
    D. a filmstrip

Use this information from a periodical index to answer questions 22, 23 and 24.

ASTRONAUTS
Astronauts in business. N. A. Martin. il Duns 100:42-6 D '72
Comedown from the moon; what has happened to the astronauts. H. Muson. il N Y Times Mag p37+ D 3 '72
Greening of the astronauts. il Time 100:43 D 11 '72
Why more astronauts are hanging up their space suits. il U.S. News 3:25-6 D 11 '72
See also
Women as astronauts
Clothing
Total story of Gemini; space suit. il Space World I-12-108:25 D '72

22. In the example above from a periodical index, how many articles are listed which give information on astronauts?

    A. 3
    B. 4
    C. 5
    D. 6

23. In the example above from a periodical index, on what page does the article written by N.A. Martin begin?

    A. 37
    B. 42
    C. 72
    D. 100

24. In the example above from a periodical index, the information *Women as astronauts* is:

    A. a footnote
    B. the title of an article
    C. a bibliography
    D. a subject heading

25. Which of the following groups of information must you know in order to find a certain article in a magazine in the media center?

    A. name of the magazine, title of the article
    B. name of the magazine, title of the article, date of the magazine
    C. name of the magazine, title of the article, author of the article
    D. name of the magazine, author of the article, page where the article begins

—4—

26. Information published by the United States Government is indexed in the:

    A. *Reader's Guide to Periodical Literature*
    B. *Monthly Catalog*
    C. *New York Times Index*
    D. *Statesman's Yearbook*

27. If the guide words on a dictionary page are **MILL** and **MINGLE,** which one of the following words would be on that same page?

    A. mile
    B. mind
    C. must
    D. master

28. The following information is given at the end of an article on *Nuclear Energy* in an encyclopedia. What does it mean?

> See: *Nuclear Power; Atomic Science;*
>   *The Atom; Bombs and Power*

    A. There are other articles related to *nuclear energy* in the encyclopedia
    B. *The Atom* is a subheading of *Nuclear Power* and *Atomic Science.*
    C. *Nuclear energy* is not a very important topic
    D. The encyclopedia is not alphabetically arranged

Use this sample Index to answer questions 29 and 30.

Complete Horse Book

Bridle 95-101, 96, 99, 144-47, 145,
    see also Bit
Bucking 298-99

C
Colts, 284-96
    driving in long reins 292-93
    obedience training 295
    riding, 294
Cow Pony; see Domestic Horses
Curb (injury), 164

D
Dealers, 88, 93
Dismounting 174, 194
Domestic Horses 48
Drill, close-order 242, 252
    mounted 241-54
    open order 242, 246, 252, 254

29. In the example above information on *open order drill* will probably be found on which page?

    A. 88
    B. 164
    C. 242
    D. 292

30. In the example above, if you were interested in *cow ponies*, what page would you look for?

    A. 48
    B. 164
    C. 294
    D. none of these

Use the following sample Table of Contents to answer questions 31 and 32.

MOON MISSION

31. In the example above, a map of the moon's surface will be on page:

    A. 6
    B. 61
    C. 95
    D. 97

32. In the example above, an alphabetical key to the information in this book will be found on page:

    A. 93
    B. 95
    C. 97
    D. 103

33. Which one of the following pieces of media equipment can be used to show a picture in a book to the whole class?

    A. opaque projector
    B. filmstrip projector
    C. movie projector
    D. overhead projector

34. What are the speeds commonly found on record players?

    A. 16, 45, 78
    B. 33 1/3, 45, 78
    C. 30, 60, 90
    D. 16 1/2, 27, 81

35. What type of media is used on this type of equipment?

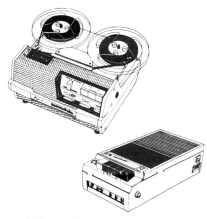

    A. transparencies
    B. 8mm films
    C. filmstrips
    D. audio tapes

36. What type of media is used on this type of equipment?

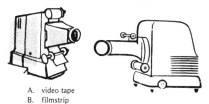

    A. video tape
    B. filmstrip
    C. cassette tape
    D. 16mm film

Use these sentences to answer questions 37 and 38.

Feeding a sick dog is a personal matter
and can be decided only by the condition
of the patient. A feeding program must
be recommended by your veterinarian
after diagnosis of the disease.

37. In the sentences above, what is the main idea or key
phrase?

   A. condition of the patient
   B. feeding a sick dog
   C. a personal matter
   D. diagnosis of the disease

38. In the sentences above, what does the word "patient"
in the first sentence refer to?

   A. the veterinarian
   B. the dog's owner
   C. the dog
   D. the disease

39. Which of the following should you do first in order to
prepare an illustrated speech on a topic you do not
know anything about?

   A. make charts and graphs
   B. outline your topic
   C. use an encyclopedia
   D. summarize the main ideas

40. The following are steps a student might use to find
information on a brand new science discovery. Which
step will probably have information on this new topic?

   A. the science textbook
   B. the almanac
   C. the periodical index
   D. the science encyclopedia

41. Which of the following series of events would be the
second thing to happen before you could take a
photograph of a turtle?

   A. focus the camera
   B. buy the film
   C. develop the film
   D. put the film in the camera

Use this picture to answer question 42.

Waste from this factory is dumped into a nearby river

42. According to this picture, which of the following
statements is correct?

   A. this factory employs more than 1,000 people
   B. this factory is a source of water pollution
   C. factory smoke is made from water vapor
   D. factories are responsible for most of the
      pollution in this country

Use this picture to answer question 43.

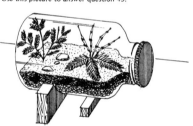

43. According to this picture of a terrarium, which of the
following statements is correct?

   A. a dark jar should be used to keep light from
      burning the plants
   B. the lid of the terrarium should be taken off for
      2 hours each day
   C. terrariums need to be watered every day
   D. large jars can be used to make a terrarium

44. Three of the following pieces of information are similar to each other; one is not. Which of the following pieces of information does not belong with the others?

   A. audio tapes can be made in the classroom
   B. old film can be bleached and reused by students
   C. 35mm slides can be made by hand without a camera
   D. overhead transparencies can be written on with permanent markers.

45. Which of the following sections of a newspaper lists jobs which are available?

   A. editorial
   B. classified
   C. society
   D. front page

46. Which of the following types of newspapers is most likely to include an article about the new television equipment at your school?

   A. daily national newspaper
   B. monthly national newspaper
   C. daily regional newspaper
   D. weekly local newspaper

47. Charts and graphs can be made by using:

   A. a record player
   B. a tape recorder
   C. a cassette recorder
   D. an overhead projector

48. The way to record a somersault for immediate play-back is to use:

   A. 16mm film equipment
   B. super 8mm equipment
   C. video tape equipment
   D. audio tape equipment

49. Slides can be made by all of the following ways EXCEPT:

   A. using a microphone
   B. using a 35mm camera
   C. writing on clear film
   D. using a copy stand

50. Which of the following could NOT be done in most school media centers?

   A. make a chart or map
   B. record a story on an audio tape
   C. make an overhead transparency
   D. make a phonograph record

51. What part of a science project lists all the information sources you used to make your report?

   A. the legend
   B. the bibliography
   C. the introduction
   D. the experiment

52. Which one of the following is a bibliography entry for a book?

   A. Wenger, Gene. "Early Cooking," page 156.
   B. "Early Cooking," Wenger, Gene. Boston: Brown, 1968.
   C. Wenger, Gene. Early Cooking, Boston: Brown, 1968.
   D. Early Cooking, by Gene Wenger, Boston: 1968.

53. New Styles for Old Hats is an article by James Love. It appeared in June 16, 1976 of News Report Magazine on page 60, 61, and 62. Which one of the following is the proper way to list this information at the end of a report?

   A. "New Styles for old Hats," June 16, 1976 News Report Magazine. page 60-62.
   B. Love, James. "New styles for old hats," News Report Magazine, June 16, 1976, p-60-62.
   C. Love, James. News Report Magazine. page 60.
   D. News Report Magazine, "New styles for old hats," by James Love. June 16, 1976, p.60-62.

1. CHECK YOUR ANSWERS.
2. TURN IN TEST BOOKLET AND ANSWER SHEET.

THE LIBRARY SKILLS TEST:
HELPING TO SET BENCHMARKS

Eileen Dubin
Northern Illinois University Library

Librarians in two recent surveys, one done by the Virginia Library Association and the other under the auspices of the American Library Association — Library Instruction Round Table, have identified the library skills they would like college freshmen to possess. Although the two surveys were slightly different, the responses were strikingly similar. Table 1 identifies in priority order the skills librarians participating in each of these surveys have identified as desirable in college freshmen.

The library skills identified in both surveys as most desired are effective use of the card catalog, correct use and interpretation of periodical indexes, effective use of common reference tools, understanding of the research process, and ability to articulate a reference question to a librarian.

To what extent college freshmen in the United States have these skills is not really known. There are no systematic data and without data there is no reliable basis for formulating systematic programs of instruction. As Hacker and Rutstein, reference librarians at Colorado State University, note, "There exist few gauges to measure success or failure of library instruction programs and that without standardized tests, librarians rely for the most part on attitudinal responses, an inefficient means of measurement."[3]

Toward the end of 1977 the Illinois Academic College and Research Libraries (IACRL), a section of the Illinois Library Association, established a Bibliographic Instruction Committee. At the initial meeting of this committee, members identified the need for a standardized test to assess the library skills of college freshmen. The committee felt that a test could be used to identify student weaknesses and strengths and, in some situations, to determine the effectiveness of library instruction. Indeed, one of the test's main functions might be to help establish standards. Finally, it might be useful in efforts to prove to university and library administrators the need for well-defined instruction programs.

With a view to establishing guidelines for library instruction and

TABLE 1

Virginia Library Association Survey
Basic Library Skills in order of their importance[1]

1   Effectively use the card catalog

2   Correctly use a periodical index and interpret the citation

3   Effectively use common reference tools such as almanacs, atlases, etc.

4   Effectively articulate a reference question to a librarian

5   Properly recognize and use microforms

6   Understand the purpose of library classification systems

LIRT
Basic Library Skills in order of their importance[2]

1   Use the card catalog

2   Identify and use a relevant periodical index and interpret the citations

3   Understand the process of doing research for a paper

4   Use common reference tools such as almanacs, atlases, etc.

5   Understand the utility of information in any sort of problem solving

6   Understand the arrangement of books in a library's classification system

7   Understand basic library terminology

8   Articulate a reference question to a librarian

9   Recognize and use microforms

10   Distinguish bibliographic form in footnotes

11   Find and use government documents

12   Recognize parts of a book

measuring benchmarks of achievement, the committee decided it should test knowledge of current terminology, the card catalog, classification systems, filing, parts of a book, indexes, reference tools, and bibliographic forms used in libraries and learning resource center. Thus, even before the ALA-LIRT and Virginia Library Association surveys, the ILA Bibliographic Instruction Committee identified as useful library skills most of the elements librarians responding to those surveys would think students should know. Rightly or wrongly, the committee felt it might be a mistake to use their test to evaluate command of research process. Firstly, since a number of alternative research strategies are valid, any instrument which assumed some as preferable might be regarded as biased. Secondly, beyond elementary strategies, research process is discipline-bound. While it is possible to evaluate student command of search strategies in specific (or related) disciplines, the committee believed the basic IACRL test was the wrong instrument for that purpose.

Finally, for convenience, the IACRL committee also agreed that their test should be one that can be administered in thirty minutes or less.

In 1978, the first draft of the committee's Library Skills Test was completed. It was tested in the fall of 1979 on students at a number of academic institutions in Illinois. Also, at this time a group of Illinois high school librarians reviewed the test and made valuable suggestions. The results obtained from the pilot project and the comments received from the school librarians led to a fine-tuning of the test and its publication by Scholastic Testing Services in 1980.

The test is designed to locate students' strengths and weaknesses in using the library. It will determine whether students have the necessary vocabulary and the mastery of basic tools. The committee believes that students not possessing those skills cannot understand a "strategy" or "process" for using a library.

The test can be used in grades 7 through 12, as well as for college freshmen. College freshmen norms already have been developed by Scholastic Testing Services in Illinois, in cooperation with the IACRL Bibliographic Instruction Committee. National norms fo grades 7 through 12 are expected to be completed by the fall of 1981.

In establishing the college norms a sample of 1,200 college students in Illinois was selected from the following colleges and universities:

Private Colleges

Aurora College	50
Elmhurst College	100

Community Colleges
Carl Sandburg College   100
Kishwaukee College   100
Lincoln Land Community College   100
Moraine Valley Community College   100
Oakton College   50

State Universities
Illinois State University   100
Northeastern Illinois University   150
Northern Illinois University   200
Western Illinois University   150

Total: 1,200

Included in this group are small private colleges, community colleges and state universities. It was thought that a more representative group of Illinois students would be found at these institutions than at some of the well-known private institutions in Illinois that recruit nationally from elite populations.

The study focused on college freshmen, although a few sophomores were included in several of the test populations. The students in each institution represented a sample from that institution, either (a) because the entire freshman class was tested from which a random sample of answer sheets was drawn, or (b) because a sample of freshman English classes was tested from which a random sample of answer sheets was drawn.

An Instructional Needs Analysis also known as a "rights analysis," or "item analysis," appears in Table 2. This analysis shows the percent of the 1,200 students marking each item correctly.

Clearly, 96% of the students tested knew the purpose served by a reference or information desk; 98% identified the author and publisher of a book from a subject entry card, 95% knew what a preface is, and 97% identified the subject heading of a newspaper article cited in the *New York Times Index*.

By way of contrast, only 50% knew the definition of an abstract. Only 35% were able to place a book properly on the shelf between the correct Library of Congress call numbers. Although 97% of the students identified the subject of a newspaper article from the *New York Times Index*, only 51% were able to tell the page on which that article would be found. Only 47% were able to distinguish bibliographic forms, isolate magazine or journal articles from a group of citations, or separate book entries from a similar grouping.

The results of the ILA test are similar in some respects to the results of the Ohio School Library Media Test, which has been used on

TABLE 2

INSTRUCTIONAL NEEDS ANALYSIS

PERCENT--CORRECT BY ITEM
ILLINOIS STUDENTS

PART I. LIBRARY TERMINOLOGY
1.	"Periodical"	90%
2.	"Bibliography"	79%
3.	"Index"	64%
4.	"Biography"	73%
5.	"Abstract"	50%
6.	"Reserve Material"	73%
7.	"Circulation Desk"	91%
8.	"Reference or Information Desk"	96%
9.	"Vertical or Pamphlet File"	75%
10.	"Microform"	90%
11.	"Audiovisual Materials"	94%
12.	"Autobiography"	85%

PART II. CATALOG CARDS
13.	Publisher of the book	98%
14.	Author of the book	98%
15.	Subject of the book	65%
16.	Title of the book	65%
17.	Publication date of the book	85%
18.	Call number of the book	89%
19.	Headings on cards	63%

PART III. CALL NUMBERS
20.	Dewey Decimal System	86%
21.	Dewey Decimal System	89%
22.	Library of Congress System	35%
23.	Library of Congress System	80%

PART IV. PARTS OF A BOOK
24.	Title page	76%
25.	Table of contents	88%
26.	Glossary	88%
27.	Preface	95%
28.	Footnote	85%
29.	Index	56%

PART V. INDEXES
30.	Number of references	66%
31.	Cross references	82%
32.	Title of a periodical	75%
33.	Abbreviations	89%
34.	Page numbers	92%
35.	Volume of a periodical	86%
36.	N.Y. Times: Subject headings	97%
37.	N.Y. Times: Page numbers	51%
38.	N.Y. Times: Column numbers	54%
39.	N.Y. Times: Dates	85%

PART VI. REFERENCE SOURCES
40.	A thesaurus	58%
41.	An unabridged dictionary	64%
42.	An encyclopedia	87%
43.	A periodical index	84%

PART VII. BIBLIOGRAPHIC FORMS
44.	Magazine (journal) articles	46%
45.	Books; parts of books	47%

the pre-collegiate level, grades 5 through 12. Both tests reveal weakness in understanding classification systems (whether Dewey or Library of Congress), identifying various types of catalog cards (particularly subject and title cards), using a periodical index, and deciphering bibliographic forms. In general, the students showed strength in understanding library terminology although the term "abstract" caused difficulty for half of the Illinois students and the term "biography" caused some problems for Ohio students. Results of the Ohio test show that upper grade students learn to place Dewey numbers in proper order, but they have trouble identifying which Dewey classification sections are associated with which broad subject areas.

In the Illinois study student raw scores ranged from a low of 7 to a high of 45. Only ten of the 1,200 students attained a perfect raw score of 45. The median score was 35.

Norms for this particular group of students are shown in Table 3. The norms table shows percentile-rank scores and stanine scores for the distribution of raw scores.

The mean of this Illinois study was 34.6, with a standard deviation of 6.1. Alpha (reliability) coefficients for the eleven colleges ranged from .630 to .833 with a median of .777. The alpha coefficient for the eleven colleges combined was .833, which yielded a standard error of measurement of 2.48 raw score points (N=1200).

Members of the ILA Bibliographic Instruction Committee suggest the follow score interpretations, which later may be modified in light of other experience.

College students scoring in the 40–45 range can be expected to understand library vocabulary and properly use basic tools. It is likely that even these students might benefit from instruction on strategies in using information sources.

College students scoring in the 33–39 range probably will need special help when working on other than routine assignments.

College students scoring below 33 cannot be expected to function effectively in the library.

Librarians responding to the LIRT and Virginia Library Associaton surveys both raise the question of the transferability of library skills from one kind of library to another. The Virginia Library Association specifically asks, "Are we teaching people to act independently to locate information, or are we teaching them mechanical procedures applicable only to our own particular library?"

The problem of transferability has several dimensions. One concerns the quality of instruction. As J.P. Nordling notes, elementary and high school students often "seem unable to integrate what they have learned about the library . . . into their research and study needs."[4] How many a university librarian has had the same complaint!

TABLE 3

STUDENT NORMS
–ILLINOIS COLLEGE STUDENTS–

Raw Score	Percentile Rank	Stanine
45	99	9
44	99	9
43	98	9
42	94	8
41	90	8
40	84	7
39	78	7
38	71	6
37	64	6
36	57	5
35	49	5
34	43	5
33	38	4
32	31	4
31	26	4
30	22	3
29	18	3
28	15	3
27	12	3
26	9	2
25	8	2
24	7	2
23	6	2
22	5	2
21	4	1
20	3	1
19	2	1
18	2	1
17	1	1
16	1	1
1–15	1	1

Mean=34.6; Media Score=35; SD=6.1; Chance Score=11; Alpha Coefficient=.833; SE meas=2.48; (N=1200)

Ms. Nordling's suggestion for remedying this condition is that library instruction be integrated into the curriculum. While that is today a popular proposal, it is more easily preached than implemented, largely because the training of the librarian and the teacher have been disparate. The library plays a very small role in teacher education programs, and in university subject matter courses, very few instructors know or care whether their students have mastered the library even in their respective disciplines. In relatively few university courses are students expected to reach out much beyond the reserve reading list. Even in elementary English courses devoted to research writing very often the student is expected to write a paper based on sources contained within an edited reader.

On the other hand, while the librarians may have a subject master's degree in addition to an M.L.S., the university librarian is likely to be insulated from instructional departments by a variety of institutional factors, not the least of which is the "academic freedom" of the instructor who does not welcome another intruding into his domain. While the integration of library instruction at the university level may occur here and there, it runs contrary to the notion of separate "cost centers," administrative decentralization, and jurisdictional jealousies, the tendency of each unit to husband scarce resources and to jettison costly, experimental or otherwise innovative courses — particularly "team taught" ones — in times of financial stringency.

Another dimension of transferability concerns the different levels of sophistication of libraries at the elementary, secondary, college and university levels and the size and quality of collections in public libraries. This issue has not been explored at great length. The ILA--IACRL Library Skills Test, which holds out prospects of establishing junior high school, secondary and university norms, offers the possibility that benchmarks may be established and that these benchmarks can be treated as instructional objectives at each of the various levels. If one can assume that the learning process is cumulative, each step up the ladder of sophistication will require the transferability of skills learned at a lower level.

NOTES

1. Virginia Library Association. Library Instruction Survey I: Librarian. 1981.

2. ALA--LIRT National Programs Study Task Force. Library Instruction Survey. 1981.

3. B.L. Hacker and J.S. Rutstein, "Educating Large Numbers of Users in University Libraries: An Analysis and Case Study," John Lubans, Jr., ed., *Progress in Educating the Library User* (New York: R.R. Bowker Company, 1978), 105.

4. J.S. Nordling, "The High School Library and the Classroom: Closing the Gap," *ibid.*, p45.

LIBRARY SKILLS TESTS:
A DEFENSE AND CRITIQUE

Anne Roberts
State University of New York at Albany

I have certainly been able to identify with all of our speakers: Joyce Merriam and her comments on high school and college library instruction skills and the repetitiveness of both; Mary Biggs and her expertise in mistakes — I have made them all; Ann Irving and her words on how people learn individually and how librarians need to get at the teachers; Anne Hyland and her concerns about accountability both from the parents and principals; and Eileen Dubin and her remarks on tests as benchmarks for library instruction skills. We all want our users to accomplish the same ends: to use the library effectively and efficiently.

The topic for this year's LOEX Conference seems appropriate, since it is evident from library literature and attendance at library instruction conferences for the last few years that school librarians want to connect with the library instruction movement that has been so active within academic libraries over the past ten to fifteen years. At SUNY–Albany this connection has come about because of our response to the high school students coming to the University Libraries with detailed and complicated search problems at times when we are not sufficiently staffed to handle all of them. When the library instruction movement started, it got its impetus from academic librarians in the field, and most conferences and articles dealt with concerns mainly relating to academic libraries: how to set up and organize programs; how to relate to the academic classroom teaching faculty; how to teach college librarians to teach; how to prepare slide/tapes and videotapes; and how to get administrative support for the programs. But in the late 1970s a dialogue began between academic librarians and elementary and school and high school librarians. (In New York State it was in Syracuse at a 1977 workshop sponsored by the New York Library Instruction Clearinghouse.) The school librarians wanted to know why college students still didn't know how to use the library and its tools, since they had been giving them library instruction. The concerns of school librarians are the same as those of academic librarians, and perhaps the methods are similar also. School librarians and academic librarians share, not only concerns, but strategies and techniques as well. We use the same skills to meet the same ends, and we can all imagine each other in our different libraries. School librarians have their days measured out by markings of the various class periods, usually by ringing bells; they often have a greater degree of collegiality with the classroom teachers than the academic librarians, since there are fewer high school librarians in each school. Along with this, school libraries may have more autonomy and more authority. School librarians also have captive audiences, and at times the hectic periods are followed by slower periods; there are the long summer vacations and vacation breaks as well as the shorter day that academic librarians sometimes envy. On the other hand, in stringent times and because of the nature of their work, school librarians cannot always get to conferences such as this one, or even a chance to visit other school libraries. I found it heartening to read of the first conference of school librarians in Louisville, Kentucky this year where some 2,549 librarians met with a clearcut active platform of goals for the American Association of School Librarians. I also had two school librarians taking a graduate course in library instruction with me at SUNY–Albany, and I was impressed about how articulate they were and how committed they were to library instruction and the needs of their students. Academic librarians do not have the necessarily strict demarcation of their days, but there are the busy and slow periods and the varied schedules of early morning or late evening and weekend hours to contend with.

What I would like to stress is how similar we are: both school and academic librarians are more alike than not, and the dialogue between us has been going on for a long time. We must both contend with the mass learning for large groups as well as the personal individualized learning. We must grapple with the new changes in the curriculum which places new demands on the library's resources, both in materials and in staff. One particular area where I think we share similar concerns is in the area of testing. It is interesting to look at the various definitions of the word; to test means examination or trial by the cupel for refining precious metals (a cupel being an earthen vessel); any critical examination or decisive trial; the means of trial, the subjection to conditions that show the real character of the person or thing in a particular fashion; a touchstone, a standard, a procedure or a reaction; and in education, any series of questions or exercises or other means of measuring the skill, knowledge, intelligence, capacities, or aptitudes of an individual or group. School librarians have been involved in the area of testing, perhaps more than academic librarians. We have heard why Anne Hyland and Eileen Dubin decided to write their own tests, how they are used, and what is done with the results. I will talk about tests for library instruction, discuss the Feagley test, comment on all three tests, and share with you my opinions of tests and library instruction in general.

One of the biggest problems in the area of testing is the giving of clear directions or instructions for taking the test. And there is strong evidence to suggest that unclear directions or poor direction-giving is one of the biggest problems within library instruction. Writing clear, objective, simple, and understandable directions is not an easy task. My graduate students in my course learn this when they set out to do their first assignment, a self-guided walking tour of a library. Both long-time practicing librarians and library school students alike discover how difficult it is to give clear directions.

General testing experts in the field of educational and psychological testing tell us that testing is used to give students feedback and to evaluate concepts and skills; not to evaluate student performances or knowledge of tools. In structuring tests they tell us we should relate the items to our objectives. They also tell us that essay tests are best for testing concepts and comprehension, and that objective or short answer tests are hard to use to measure anything; multiple choice tests give the greatest variety and provide more validity than the objective or short answer tests.

Most library instruction pre-tests try and find out what the students don't know, rather than what they do know. Library definitions, abbreviations, library terms, and individual reference tools are our favorites for us to write and to devise tests for. Pre-tests can be useful, mainly for us, the instruction librarians, because we are then made aware of the fact that, although we are speaking English, the library language we are speaking is a foreign language to the students we are instructing in the ways of the library. For most people, using a library for basic functions really doesn't require that they know the meanings of library terms and the library definitions and what the abbreviations stand for. As an example, when you are visiting a foreign country, you can get around fairly easily if you know a few phrases; you don't really have to be conversant in the language, or know it intimately to get to your destination, or to find housing and food. If you really want to understand the lives of the people and their culture, however, you must speak and understand the language. This summer in Mexico travelling with several assorted adults and children, the only two phrases we absolutely depended on were "where is" and "how much." Perhaps we instruction librarians have been trying to get our students to speak and understand the library language when just one or two phrases are in order. In addition to terms like: "serial," "bibliography," "anthology," and "annotation," students often have difficulty with library procedures if they haven't done them yet. To locate books on the shelf; to institute a save, a hold, or a recall; or to initiate an interlibrary loan request, may be confusing the first time you do it. Classification schemes, be they Library of Congress or Dewey, and our library filing rules, whether letter-by-letter or word-by-word, can all be confusing to the first time library user.

The Feagley test, named after its principal author, Ethel M. Feagley, of Teachers College, Columbia University, written in the 1950s, was made at a time when there were basic required courses, such as the history of western civilization, world literature, English composition, and basic science courses. Most colleges and universities did require their students to take certain courses, so that a core of knowledge to be mastered was presupposed. In essence, it was a era of requirements. This assumption is evident in the Feagley test, for it clearly tried to discover to what extent, and what areas, college freshmen needed instruction in using the resources of the college library. The test also attempted to help students recognize that they needed help, and it was designed to provide the necessary information to the librarians giving the test so they in turn could develop and plan a program of library instruction based on the test results, and fitted to the needs of the students. It was all very neat and orderly. The Feagley test has stood up well over the years, and it is still one of the best of its type, even though it is dated, selective, and doesn't encompass many of the findings of the current library instruction movement such as the search strategy concept. Nevertheless, countless librarians have relied on it over the years, and have even used it as a model for their own library instruction tests. The Feagley test went through several revisions as the librarians at Teachers College experimented with it for five years, and observed students taking it from 1950 to 1955. It went through three revisions, and was reviewed in the *Mental Measurements Yearbooks* of Oscar Buros. The first two reviewers, Janet G. Afflerbach, editor of the Professional Examination Service, and Lois G. Afflerbach, Serials Librarian at Queens College, note that the Feagley test gives a two-way assessment, backwards at the high school training, and forwards to the college library program: emphasizing the card catalog, specific reference tools, and library terms. They point out that no dictionary or encyclopedia questions are presented. The test itself consists of nine parts: matching terms, parts of a catalog card, standard subject headings (broad vs. subdivisions), alphabetizing according to filing rules, English literature reference books, general reference tools, general indexes, interpreting a periodical citation, and abbreviations and their meanings. These reviewers feel that the test was initially well-received, and that it will do what it says it will. The next reviewer, J. Wayne Wrightstone, Director of Educational

Resources of the New York Public Schools, faults the test on not having data for itself on reliability, validity, and norms, and therefore he concludes that the test cannot be considered as a standardized one. He does, however, laud the authors of the Feagley test for attempting to approximate real library situations in their use of actual examples, and in their citation of the more commonly used library sources. Wrightstone feels that the test would help in counseling students to use the library and its resources, and points out the fact that the test was carried out to determine whether or not students had to take basic library instruction in college or be waived from it, much like the 1950s requirement many colleges had for English composition. A third reviewer, Morey J. Wantman, of the Educational Testing Service at Princeton, comments that the test contains too many options. He does agree that the Feagley test is probably better than an informal test individual librarians might design, since it does give us some concrete information to help instruct students in the use of libraries.

I must confess that when I was developing my own instruction program, particularly the basic library research credit course, I went to the Feagley test, and used it as a model for my own pre-test. Since then I have developed my own pre-test which tests more exactly what I teach in my course. Why did I go to the Feagley test for a resource? I guess I felt somewhat reassured that the Feagley test had lasted for awhile and therefore must be good; also that the Teachers College must have known what it was doing, and what did I know about testing or pre-tests for library instruction anyway? The Feagley test helped me when I needed it, and it was only after I had taught my credit course for several terms that I began to realize how little relationship the Feagley test bore to what I was actually teaching. I was concentrating on the search strategy, dealing with individual students and their particular subjects, and was trying to get at the structure of the literature of the areas or fields that the individual students were writing their topics in. Nonetheless, I still had them compile a bibliography, and do other general activities in the library that I felt they should know about. I discovered that they needed to know how books were arranged on the shelf, how they were filed in the card catalog, how to determine which items were subject headings, and how to decipher a periodical index entry, and even how to charge out a book from circulation. So, I can see why individual librarians do want to develop their own tests.

The Ohio test, for grades four through twelve, claims to measure what students know about using media centers, and therefore can be used as both a pre-test and post-test. Anne Hyland uses Bloom's taxonomy for identifying the five skill areas she is testing, and focuses on student throught processes. I had trouble taking her test; I felt she was testing what she felt the students should know, and not necessarily what the students themselves really needed to know. I asked my two high school librarians to take both the Ohio test and the Illinois test and go over each test item in light of their long experiences with high school students and library instruction. Both Judith Lott and Mary Anne Lanni have had considerable experience as high school librarians/media specialists, and are keenly interested in library instruction for high school students. They both felt that the format of the Ohio test was good, but that some of the questions might be confusing, and even misleading to students. They felt the test covered the areas of a media center in very specific terms and not all media centers would be so arranged.

The Illinois test of Eileen Dubin appealed to all three of us a bit more, perhaps because it felt more comfortable and was more like the Feagley test. (I should add that the three of us are approximately the same age and that may have some bearing on our test preferences as well.) Both of the high school librarians felt this test could be used at more levels within the grades, if you had honors students for instance, and they like the division of parts. The test questions seemed clearer and more general library skills were tested. An attempt at getting high school students into research projects was made in this test and the high school librarians liked that aspect of the test. One high school librarian did not have one of the tools, *Biography Index*, so that was a problem for her. Perhaps our inclination for the Illinois test over the Ohio test was that it seems to address general skills. The Illinois test, like the Feagley test, was compiled by a group of people, rather than only one person. Often there is virtue in numbers, for what one person feels worked, another may question, and in that process some of the ambiguities may be eliminated.

I will now come back to my original statement and say that I think we instruction librarians test for library skills for negative reasons: to find out what students don't know that we think they should know. I have mentioned the difficulty we have with unclear directions. Experience for learners is important; as John Dewey pointed out, we can learn by doing. If we instruction librarians are going to test, we must test to our own teaching objectives. Too often we latch on to existing tests and use them, sometimes with unfortunate results, since the tests we choose bear little relationship to what we are trying to teach. I think that if we are going to test, we are better off devising our own tests like Anne Hyland and Eileen Dubin did since our teaching objectives may differ from each other according to our own individual situations and our users.

But I will go further, and state that perhaps we should consider not testing at all in library instruction, at least not as we have been doing in the past. I think we must pay more attention to individualized learning in library instruction, and take a cue from the research that is currently being done on how people learn to read and to write. We need to work closely with the reading laboratories and the writing centers of our institutions. For learning may be invisible and not apparent to the observer. In order to really know how people think, we may have to get at this invisible process through the more visible ones of reading and writing. I will further argue that we may have been going about our library instruction in the wrong way. What hard tangible evidence do we really have that all of our programs and activities in library instruction have worked? Have we just erected another system of barriers between the users and the library? Perhaps we have only gotten at part of the problem if at all; we may only have influenced our students in the affective domain, and not in the cognitive domain. We may have made our users feel better about themselves but not have made them learn more about using libraries. If any real learning of library skills occurred, it was a happy coincidence or by-product perhaps. We may have made things worse by our proclivity towards organizing information into such complex access systems which we call library instruction. And finally, has testing really been an evaluation tool for library instruction, or has testing been a hindrance?

BIBLIOGRAPHY

Anastasi, Anne. *Psychological Testing*. New York: Macmillan, 1976.

Buros, Oscar. *The Fifth Mental Measurements Yearbook*. Highland Park, New Jersey: The Gryphon Press, 1959.

------------------. *The Sixth Mental Measurements Yearbook*. Highland Park, New Jersey: The Gryphon Press, 1965.

Hawes, Gene. *Educational Testing for the Millions*. New York: McGraw--Hill, 1964.

Kline, Paul. *Psychological Testing: The Measurement of Intelligence, Ability, and Personality*. London: Malaby Press, 1976.

Perkins, Ralph. *The Prospective Teacher's Knowledge of Library Fundamentals*. New York: Scarecrow Press, 1965. This book has a section on "The Feagley Library Orientation Test for College Freshmen," pp. 153--193.

Werking, Richard Hume. "Evaluating Bibliographic Education" in *Library Trends*, 29:153--172 (Summer 1980).

----------------------------. "The Place of Evaluation in Bibliographic Education" in *Proceedings from the Southeastern Conference on Approaches to Bibliographic Instruction*. Charleston: 1978.

DEVELOPING STATEWIDE LIBRARY INSTRUCTION STANDARDS: RATIONALE AND PRELIMINARY STEPS

Frederick R. Reenstjerna
Roanoke VA Public Library: Hollins Branch

It has been said that we are living in the "Information Age;" the dominant feature of our society is the generation and distribution of information. Public libraries undoubtedly are the MASH units of our informational society. We get all sorts of clients with all sorts of information needs, and we must respond to the clients and the needs as best we can. To pursue the MASH analogy, let me say that as I view this audience, I feel like Dr. Hawkeye Pierce addressing a convention of Dr. Charles Winchesters — our backgrounds are decidedly different.

I have attempted to locate supporting bibliographic material on my topic, but results were generally fruitless. An article in John Lubans' *Progress in Educating the Library User* mentioned that only three citations were located, and one was in Russian.[1] My own search of subsequent issues of *Library Literature* revealed only two additional articles on public-library user instruction, and one of those was the essay by Sheryl Anspaugh in the aforementioned collection by John Lubans. Unfortunately, after I had written this paper, I was supplied by Project LOEX with a bibliography of materials on public-library user instruction, including unpublished materials and ERIC documents. At this stage, I shall have to follow a motto that I once read: "My mind is made up; don't confuse me with facts." I hope that my experiences and opinions will square with the facts cited in other works; I feel that there is a consensus on basic issues.

Let me begin by setting the stage with some representative cases in an afternoon at my library, the Hollins Branch of the Roanoke County Public Library. An elderly couple approach the reference desk with bottles of prescription medication, asking how they can find out more about the pills their physician has prescribed. After them, a young man who has a job interview the next morning asks for help in locating background information about the interviewing firm. Next, I notice a tenth-grader checking out a book on amphibians. Further questioning reveals, that, once again, the "frog-systems" report project has been assigned to the tenth grade at the

FIGURE 1

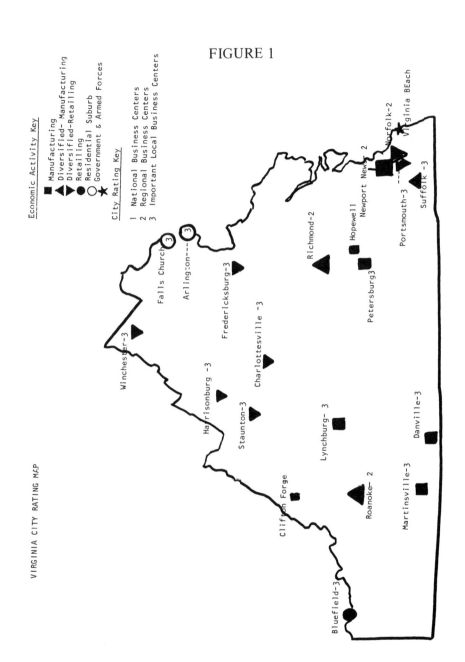

VIRGINIA CITY RATING MAP

Economic Activity Key
■ Manufacturing
◀ Diversified- Manufacturing
▶ Diversified-Retailing
● Retailing
○ Residential Suburb
★ Government & Armed Forces

City Rating Key
1 National Business Centers
2 Regional Business Centers
3 Important Local Business Centers

Falls Church 3
Arlington---3
Winchester-3
Fredericksburg-3
Harrisonburg -3
Charlottesville -3
Staunton-3
Lynchburg- 3
Clifton Forge
Roanoke- 2
Martinsville-3
Danville-3
Bluefield-3
Richmond-2
Hopewell
Petersburg3
Newport News 2
Portsmouth-3
Norfolk-2
Virginia BEach
Suffolk -3

neighboring high school. I hastily scoop up all books illustrating frog reproductive, digestive, circulatory, etc., systems, and put them on one-week circulation.

While this has been going on, an engineer from the nearby ITT plant calls with a specific-title request for a book on polymer chemistry. Amazingly, the Hollins Branch Library does not stock that particular book, but I am able to locate it in Knoxville, Tennessee. The engineer, who has a bigger telephone budget than I, calls Knoxville and asks them to hold the book pending receipt of my interlibrary loan request.

There are over eight million stories in the naked library, and these are just a few of them. All of these people required, and deserved, some form of guidance in making efficient and effective use of available resources to isolate the particular information that they needed. Whether you call it bibliographic instruction, library instruction, library orientation, or some other buzzword, is irrelevant to the needs or to the results.

You noticed in the cases cited, a variety of age and education levels among the clientele. It is impossible to delimit public-library users in the parameters available to academic and school libraries: grade, age, income level, or any other classification will not restrict the clientele. This perspective on library users is the basis for my interest in developing standards of library skills that could be applied to a diverse population.

There is a second reason to involve public libraries in the instructional process; it is the result of national demographic patterns and the economics of higher education. College officials are doing a new dance these days, called the "Off-Campus Hustle." Faced with continually-decreasing enrollments as the "baby boom" turns into the "baby bust," colleges are involving more and more older students in part-time, off-campus programs. The income from this expanded enrollment is good for the college, the prospects of "credentialization" are good for the students (everybody needs more education for advancement on the job, these days), but the instructional resources are usually poor to mediocre — when they exist at all. Libraries are often low-priority items on campus. Where the supply lines are stretched into off-campus programs, students often must forage for whatever bibliographic support is available at or near their class site.

Let me give you a typical case of off-campus activity and its impact on library resources. Figure 1 shows the Southwest Virginia market area, as described by the *Rand McNally Commercial Atlas*. Notice that Roanoke is the dominant city in this region. The highest-level state-supported educational institution in Roanoke is a two-year community college; there are two private colleges near the city, but neither is closely involved in the community.

A graduate program in business administration is offered in Roanoke by Lynchburg College, a private college in a city fifty miles to the east. Some of the students in the M.B.A. program are from Martinsville, a furniture-manufacturing city forty miles south of Roanoke.

Now, here is your sweepstakes question. A supervisor in a textile mill outside of Martinsville is enrolled in the Lynchburg College program. This semester, she is taking a course in Roanoke on personnel policy. The course is taught in a building belonging to Roanoke College, where most of the local Lynchburg College classes are given, and the professor is an official with the Appalachian Power Company. The major portion of this student's grade will come from a research paper discussing some aspect of personnel policy. The question is: who is responsible for giving this person the library orientation she needs? Further, to which library should she be oriented — Lynchburg College, Roanoke College, or some of the Martinsville public and academic libraries closer to the student's home? This student is functioning in a *de facto* intertype library network, yet no library is taking the initiative to explain to her the use of available information resources.

A third, critical aspect of library orientation in public libraries is not even addressed by the title of this conference. Your concern is with "bridging the gap from high school to college." If a person goes to work as a secretary, are they not in need of library/information orientation? The man or woman on the factory floor and assembly line needs to know how to find out about his/her job rights and responsibilities. When the emphasis in library socialization is on the "preppies," there is an implication that libraries are not germane to the lives of ordinary working folks.

I would venture a suggestion that this elitism, whether intentional or accidental, is a dangerous attitude in the 1980s. An immense army of contemporary barbarians, led by the Proposition-13 Huns, stands ready to sack most of the information/educational system on which our society is based. Now is the time to expand our clientele, not restrict it: let everyone know the advantages of access to information.

We have a penchant in the library profession for compartmentalization, perhaps it is the latent cataloger in all of us, seeking order and classification. There is a strong social-class element in our compartmentalization, also: academic librarians look down on public librarians, public librarians look down on school librarians, and everybody looks down on catalogers and children's librarians. A great amount of this division and specialization carries over into our relationships with our users, to our mutual disadvantage.

How many of you in the audience have been shopping in a

department store and, after a long search, finally located someone who is an employee of the store? After explaining your need to this person, you are told, "I'm sorry, that is not my department. You will have to talk to someone else." How did you feel — frustrated, angry, convinced of the incompetence of all clerks? Well, now, let us try the shoe on the other foot.

Imagine that you are working in a typing pool while attending night school at a junior college. You live thirty miles (round trip) from campus, and you have to write a term paper in your English class on Chaucer's *Canterbury Tales*. Within a mile of your home is a branch public library, so you stop off there on your way home from work, planning to gather materials for your paper. How would you feel when the librarian told you, "I'm sorry. We do not have anything related to school assignments here. You should go to your college library." To compound the problem, let us assume that the junior college has a policy of refusing to supply interlibrary loans for students.

Compare your feelings in the department-store case to those in this last one. If you were that secretary, would you have the sophistication to understand the distinctions among types of libraries and their collection-development philosophies? Do you, as librarians, have a similarly sophisticated knowledge of corporate organization to understand the referral from one retail clerk to another?

As I mentioned before, we cannot allow the luxury any longer of ignorance, library illiteracy, if you will, among our clientele. We must work to involve as many people as possible in the library process. We must bridge many gaps — from high school to college, from high school to the "real world" of work, and from college to special libraries. Without insuring that we are teaching students how to make these transitions, we are sealing our own fate as a profession and as institutions.

How many high-school librarians at this conference experience any use of their libraries by past or recent graduates of their schools? How many college librarians would categorize alumni use of their libraries as a "significant" percentage of library use? I submit that the bulk of your former students who are still using libraries, are visiting their local public libraries for books and information.

How many academic and school librarians at this conference have involved public libraries in their instructional programs? If you have not, ask yourselves why not. I do not believe that any of the traditional arguments for compartmentalization of library service will bear up in the harsh light of 1981's economic and political realities. Furthermore, we librarians — of all people — should be most sensitive to the social changes brought on by the amount of new information being added to the general body of knowledge. Graduates from high schools in 1981 will be at mid-career in A.D. 2003; they will get their gold watches upon retirement in the year 2028. Facility in the use of a card, microform, or on-line catalog at a high school or college library in the 1980s is not nearly as important to these people as decision-making ability — knowing which types of resources are most likely to yield the most information. We must impart an awareness of types of libraries, types of information, and experience in using as many of these types as possible while we still have the captive audience of students.

There are a number of ways in which co-operative projects can be developed between public and educational (school and academic) libraries. I have worked on two cases which I offer as examples. Working with the head of a high-school business department, I supplied resources and gave a presentation to a senior secretarial class. After explaining basic reference sources, I left with the class some older reference books for "hands-on" experience during the week. Almanacs, *Standard and Poor's*, looseleaf services, and similar books were available to the students for a week. The teacher used work sheets from her teacher's guide to develop questions for the students.

There is no way that a high school in Roanoke County, Virginia, can justify purchasing *Standard and Poor's*, the Moody directories of businesses, or looseleaf services. Yet, to function as effective executive secretaries, high-school graduates must be familiar with these resources. Unless we are content with a Catch-22 situation, we must develop co-operative programs involving all types of libraries to explain these different resources to our clients.

In another situation, I have been giving presentations to noncollege-bound high-school seniors. In a single class period, I explain to them the "non-term-paper" resources of public libraries — labor-law guides, car-repair manuals, and consumer information, which will be more important to them as workers and adults. These lectures are given specifically to the non-college-bound seniors, in an attempt to improve their perception of public library resources.

We must conclude that all libraries have something to offer a user, and that many people use different types of libraries. Perhaps we have moved away from the "floating librarian" described a decade ago by Professor Mary Lee Bundy of the University of Maryland; today we have the "floating library user." Library users have created their own networks.

This, then, is the user rationale for developing statewide library-instruction standards, a policy which we are pursuing in the Library Instruction Forum of the Virginia Library Association. We must catch up to our clientele, and adopt their broad perspective on library resources — supplanting their naivete with a better understanding of available information.

There is another reason for a more generalized approach to library instruction. One of the members of our Library Instruction Forum has observed that her high-school daughter has an absolute aversion to libraries of any kind. The reason for the daughter's reaction is that she has had so many basic library instruction classes on how to use the card catalog that she is about ready to scream. Every grade uses the same presentation, so that by high school, the cumulative effect is deadening.

We must think in terms of individuals, not in terms of masses of people grouped arbitrarily, in making users aware of library resources. An adult and one fourteen-year-old might be at the same, basic level of library literacy, while another fourteen-year-old might be at a higher level, able to understand and use more advanced tools. This is the goal of our project in Virginia: to develop standards of skills that can be applied in any situation, depending upon the user's level of competence.

Our work in this field is admittedly primitive by many measures of evaluation, but is is apparently something of a pioneer effort. People driving on paved roads may not always realize the difficulties of travel by ox-cart over dirt tracks. We are definitely at the ox-cart stage of comprehensive standards, but it is because we cannot locate any superhighways.

We have an ultimate political aim in our standards work, as well as the aim of improving library instruction. The Commonwealth of Virginia now requires a competency examination of all high school seniors; high school diplomas can be granted only upon successful completion of this test. If we in the library community can identify a set of skills that are agreed upon as fundamental needs of all high-school graduates, we have a chance of including these library skills questions on the competency examination. The name of the game these days is quantification, so we are proceeding in a manner that will document and quantify as much as possible about library skills.

To identify needed library skills, a questionnaire was developed and sent to librarians in Virginia. We asked practicing librarians to identify those skills which they thought a high-school senior or college freshman should possess. We also asked questions about the librarians' perceptions of transferability of skills — to what extent did they think skills learned in secondary school could be transferred to college or to public libraries?

The first questionnaire is being followed by a second survey, now in progress, directed toward library users. We will ask a sample of college freshmen, high school students, and public library clients to identify those library skills which they think are important. We will then try to reach a consensus of basic skills, as identified by librarians and users independently.

The first survey was mailed to approximately 450 libraries in Virginia. A total of 154 responses were received, in the following categories:

	NUMBER	PERCENT
School	81	51
Academic	38	25
Public	29	19
Special	6	5
TOTAL	154	100

A copy of the questionnaire is reproduced in Appendix I of this report. An analysis of the responses to each question, tabulated by type of library, is included in Appendix II of this report.

The results of the survey are interesting for several reasons. First, even though some, perhaps many, of the responses might seem intuitively obvious, they are obtained inductively. To the extent that they are the result of empirical research, these responses may be more valid than speculative hypotheses. Second, many more librarians supported library instruction as an abstraction than were willing or able to put into practice any institutional program. Perhaps this is an indication that a more readily available methodology should be provided, since there is apparently a receptive audience in the profession.

Additionally, several items in the questionnaire were intended to determine the background of librarians in educational methodology. These data may be used to justify more training for professionals in teaching techniques, to support their instructional roles.

On the general issue of library instruction, one hundred seven (107) librarians, or sixty-nine percent (69%) of all responding, reported that their libraries currently have a library instruction program. These programs are concentrated in school and academic libraries (80% and 82%, respectively), with only 28% of public libraries and 33% of special libraries reporting a program.

Of the total responding, only 57 librarians (37%) reported having written, specific objectives for their programs. School libraries had written objectives in 56% of the cases, academic libraries had such objectives in only 29% of cases, and no public or special libraries acknowledged written objectives. Thus, approximately half of all libraries with instructional programs have specific written objectives for those programs.

Librarians were almost unanimous in their support for special orientation programs — 93% of all respondents thought they were needed for their particular libraries. Public librarians were the least positive segment, for only 79% thought orientations to their libraries necessary. Academic, school, and special librarians were at least 95% in favor of special orientation programs for their libraries.

Reality closely matched ambition in this instance, as most school and academic librarians who felt the need for special orientation programs did indeed provide such programs. Public libraries fell farthest below: only 9 librarians reported user orientation programs, while 23 felt such activities were needed.

Three questions (numbers 13 through 15 of the questionnaire) addressed the problem of transferability of library skills. This may be one of the crucial issues in library instruction, as the theme of this conference attests.

The questionnaire did not attempt to design a measurement of transferability. Operating at a more subjective level, we asked librarians for their impressions: did they expect new users to be able to use academic or public libraries, and did they think that school library skills were transferable? The phrases "new user" and "use the library" are admittedly nebulous concepts. Respondents were asked to imagine a high school senior or college freshman as the generalized new user of academic or public libraries. Librarians were asked also to interpret "use the library" as meaning the ability to identify and manipulate the most elementary catalogs or reference tools.

A slim majority of all those responding, 51%, expected new users to be able to use an academic library. Only 27% of the sample voted no on this issue; 22% expressed no opinion.

More respondents expected new users to be able to use public libraries: 103 librarians, or 66% of the total, supported this conclusion, while only 23 (15%) did not expect new users to be able to use a public library.

When asked the extent to which secondary-school library skills were transferable, respondents thought most or all skills were transferable to academic and public libraries. Academic and school librarians had higher ratings for both of these categories; i.e., they were more certain than public or special librarians that secondary-school library skills were transferable to academic and public libraries.

Question 15, which asked for skills thought to be most difficult to transfer, produced a variety of comments. Some remarks made by librarians specified these problems, among others: special reference tools in other libraries; the many different kinds of indexes; divided catalogs; the physical size of other libraries; making the transition from Dewey to LC classifications; and an unwillingness to ask for assistance.

An important section of the survey was the ranking of library skills (Question 16). On a range of 1 to 5 (5 being most important), librarians indicated the relative importance of a list of potential skills. For all respondents, the skills were ranked in the following order:

RANK	SCORE	SKILL
1	4.71	Effectively use the card catalog
2	4.26	Correctly use a periodical index & interpret the citation
3	4.18	Effectively use common reference tools (almanacs, etc.)
4	3.87	Effectively articulate a reference question
5	3.30	Understand the purpose of library classification systems
6	2.95	Properly recognize and use microforms
7	2.67	Correctly locate the men's/women's restrooms

The score mentioned above is the mean of all responses; those skills whose averages approach 5 are more important than those scores approaching 1. The rankings of skills by particular types of librarians are given in Appendix III of this report. Among all types of libraries, it is interesting that the relative importance of these skills did not change dramatically. Particular skills might change from third to fourth rank, or seventh to sixth, but there were no major reversals. The most dramatic change was when special librarians ranked articulation of a reference question second, while that skill ranked fourth overall; there were no changes from first to seventh or vice versa. This would tend to indicate that a common instructional program is indeed feasible for all types of libraries.

Not only is such a common feasible, but it is apparently desirable — 76% of all respondents favored the development of comprehensive standards.

So, here we are on the darkling plain. It is to be hoped that our preliminary work will lead to implementation of standards of library instruction in Virginia. I hope that I have been able to help you realize something about library instruction in the "public sector," so to speak, and I hope that you have a greater understanding both of our problems and our potential for mutual service through cooperative effort.

NOTES

1. Anspaugh, Sheryl. "Public Libraries: Teaching the User?" in *Progress in Educating the Library User*, ed. by John Lubans (New York, Bowker, 1978), pp. 125--132.

2. The illustration is adapted from the *Rand McNally Commerical Atlas*, c1979.

LIBRARY INSTRUCTION QUESTIONNAIRE

LIBRARY INSTRUCTION SURVEY

NAME: (optional): _____

JOB TITLE: _____

INSTITUTION: _____

ADDRESS: _____

1. Have you ever had a formal course in library-skills orientation?
   ____ Yes   ____ No

2. Did this course include methods of instruction?
   ____ Yes   ____ No

3. Have you ever attended an in-depth workshop (3 days or more) on library skills instruction?
   ____ Yes   ____ No

4. Did this workshop include methods of instruction?
   ____ Yes   ____ No

5. Who is the co-ordinator of the library-instruction program in your institution? (Give position title) _____
   _____

6. Do you currently have a library-instruction program?
   ____ Yes   ____ No

7. Do you have written specific objectives for the library-instruction program?
   ____ Yes   ____ No

8. Is your library skills program taught in conjunction with subject-area curricula?
   ____ Yes   ____ No   ____ Does not apply

9. Do you pre-test the user on library skills?

_____ Yes _____ No

10. Do you post-test the user on library skills?

_____ Yes _____ No

11. Do you think there is a need for special orientation programs in library skills for new users of your library?

_____ Yes _____ No

12. Do you provide a user orientation program?

_____ Yes _____ No

13. Do you expect a new user to be able to use the:

a) Academic library? _____ Yes _____ No
b) Public library? _____ Yes _____ No

14. To what degree do you think library skills taught at the secondary level are transferable to a:

a) College library?
_____ Not at all transferable
_____ Some but not most skills are transferable
_____ Most but not all skills are transferable
_____ All skills are transferable

b) Public library?
_____ Not at all
_____ Some but not all
_____ Most but not all
_____ All

15. What library skills, if any, present the greatest transfer problems from secondary school libraries to:

a) Academic libraries? _____
_____

b) Public libraries? _____
_____

16. Using a score of 1 to 5 (1=low, 5=high), rank the following competencies that a user should have acquired:

_____ effectively use the card catalog
_____ effectively articulate a reference question to a librarian
_____ correctly use a periodical index and interpret the citations
_____ understand the purpose of library classification systems
_____ correctly locate the women's/men's restroom
_____ properly recognize and use microforms
_____ effectively use common reference tools such as almanacs, atlases, dictionaries, and encyclopedias

17. Do you favor the development of a comprehensive set of standards for library instruction for all types of libraries?

_____ Yes   _____ No

APPENDIX II:

TABULATION OF QUESTIONNAIRE RESPONSES

RESULTS

Responses to the questions were tabulated as follow (questions without quantifiable answers are omitted from this listing):

1. Have you ever had a formal course in library skills instruction?

RESPONSES:	YES	%	NO	%	OMITTED	%
School	35	43	46	57		
Academic	6	16	31	82	1	3
Public	3	10	26	90		
Special	2	33	4	67		
TOTAL	46	30	108	70		

2. Did this course include methods of instruction?

RESPONSES:	YES	%	NO	%	OMITTED	%
School	28	35	20	25	32	40
Academic	4	11	9	24	25	66
Public	3	10	9	31	17	59
Special	1	17	4	57	1	17
TOTAL	36	23	43	28	75	48

3. Have you ever attended an in-depth workshop on library skills instruction?

RESPONSES:	YES	%	NO	%	OMITTED	%
School	11	14	68	84	2	2
Academic	11	29	24	63	3	8
Public	3	10	25	86	1	3
Special	0	0	6	100		
TOTAL	25	16	124	80	6	4

4. *Did this workshop include methods of instruction?*

RESPONSES	YES	%	NO	%	OMITTED	%	N/A	%
School	9	11	16	20	53	65	3	4
Academic	9	24	5	13	24	63		
Public	3	10	7	24	19	66		
Special	0	0	2	33	4	67		
TOTAL	21	14	31	20	100	65	3	2

6. *Do you currently have a library instruction program?*

RESPONSES	YES	%	NO	%	OMITTED	%
School	65	80	14	17	2	2
Academic	31	82	7	18		
Public	8	28	19	66	2	7
Special	2	33	3	50	1	17
TOTAL	107	69	43	28	5	3

7. *Do you have written specific objectives for the library instruction program?*

RESPONSES	YES	%	NO	%	OMITTED	%	N/A	%
School	46	56	30	37	4	5	1	1
Academic	11	29	21	57	6	16		
Public	0	0	21	72	8	28		
Special	0	0	5	83	1	17		
TOTAL	57	37	78	50	19	12	1	1

8. *Is your library skills program taught in conjunction with subject area curricula?*

RESPONSES:	YES	%	NO	%	OMITTED	%	N/A	%
School	64	79	10	12	5	6	2	2
Academic	22	58	8	21	6	16	2	5
Public	0	0	4	14	4	14	21	72
Special	2	33	3	50	1	17		
TOTAL	89	57	25	16	16	10	25	16

9. Do you pre-test the user on library skills?

RESPONSES:	YES	%	NO	%	OMITTED	%	N/A	%
School	22	27	50	62	8	10	1	1
Academic	7	18	25	66	6	16		
Public	0	0	20	69	9	31		
Special	0	0	5	83	1	17		
TOTAL	29	19	101	65	24	15	1	1

10. Do you post-test the user on library skills?

RESPONSES:	YES	%	NO	%	OMITTED	%	N/A	%
School	52	64	24	30	4	5	1	1
Academic	17	45	14	37	7	18		
Public	1	3	18	62	10	34		
Special	0	0	5	83	1	17		
TOTAL	70	45	62	40	22	14	1	1

11. Do you think there is a need for special orientation programs in library skills for new users of your library?

RESPONSES	YES	%	NO	%	OMITTED	%
School	78	96	2	2	1	1
Academic	36	95	1	3	1	3
Public	23	79	3	10	3	10
Special	6	100				
TOTAL	144	93	6	4	5	3

12. Do you provide a user orientation program?

RESPONSES:	YES	%	NO	%	OMITTED	%	N/A	%
School	72	89	8	10	1	1		
Academic	33	87	2	5	2	5	1	3
Public	9	31	16	55	4	14		
Special	5	83	1	17				
TOTAL	119	77	28	18	7	5	1	1

13. *Do you expect a new user to be able to use the:*

a) Academic library?

RESPONSES:	YES	%	NO	%	OMITTED	%
School	48	59	17	21	16	20
Academic	21	55	13	34	4	11
Public	5	17	11	38	13	45
Special	4	67	1	17	1	17
TOTAL	79	51	42	27	34	22

b) Public library?

RESPONSES:	YES	%	NO	%	OMITTED	%	N/A	%
School	60	74	10	12	10	12	1	1
Academic	18	47	6	16	14	37		
Public	20	69	7	24	2	7		
Special	4	67			2	33		
TOTAL	103	66	23	15	28	18	1	1

14. *To what degree do you think library skills taught at the secondary level are transferable to a:*

a) College library?
1 _____ Not at all transferable
2 _____ Some but not most skills transferable
3 _____ Most but not all skills are transferable
4 _____ All skills are transferable

RESPONSES:	1	%	2	%	3	%	4	%	Omitted	%	Mean
School	0	0	16	20	25	31	39	48	1	1	3.29
Academic	2	5	9	24	11	29	14	37	2	5	3.03
Public	1	3	7	24	11	38	7	24	3	10	2.92
Special	1	17	4	67	0	0	1	17			2.17
TOTAL	4	3	37	24	47	30	61	39	6	4	3.11

b) Public library?
1 _____ Not at all transferable
2 _____ Some but not most skills are transferable
3 _____ Most but not all skills are transferable
4 _____ All skills are transferable

RESPONSES:	1	%	2	%	3	%	4	%	Omitted	%	Mean
School	0	0	11	14	27	33	42	52			3.39
Academic	1	3	3	8	12	32	11	29	11	29	3.22
Public	0	0	8	28	9	31	11	38	1	3	3.11
Special	0	0	3	50	2	33	1	17			2.67
TOTAL	1	1	25	16	51	33	65	42	12	8	3.27

16. Using a score of 1 to 5 (1=low, 5=high), rank the following competencies that a user should have acquired:

_____ *effectively use the card catalog*

RESPONSES:	1	%	2	%	3	%	4	%	5	%	Om.	%	Mean
School	2	2	0	0	1	1	3	4	73	90	2	2	4.84
Academic	1		1	3	3	3	8	9	24	24	63	0	4.42
Public	0	0	0	0	2	7	2	7	25	86	0		4.79
Special	0	0	0	0	0	0	1	17	5	83	0		4.83
TOTAL	3	2	2	1	6	4	15	10	127	82	2	1	4.71

_____ *effectively articulate a reference question to a librarian*

RESPONSES:	1	%	2	%	3	%	4	%	5	%	Om.	%	Mean
School	1	1	3	4	20	25	19	23	34	42	4	5	4.06
Academic	1	3	7	18	9	24	11	29	3	8	0		3.63
Public	2	7	5	17	4	14	7	24	10	34	1	3	3.64
Special	0	0	0	0	2	33	3	50	1	17	0		3.84
TOTAL	4	3	15	10	33	21	39	25	56	36	8	5	3.87

_____ *correctly use a periodical index & interpret the citations*

RESPONSES:	1	%	2	%	3	%	4	%	5	%	Om.	%	Mean
School	2	2	2	2	9	11	16	20	51	63	1	1	4.40
Academic	0	0	1	3	5	13	11	29	20	53	1	3	4.35
Public	1	0	2	7	9	31	9	31	9	31	0		3.86
Special	1	17	1	17	0	0	1	17	3	50	0		3.67
TOTAL	3	2	6	4	23	15	37	24	84	54	2	1	4.26

_____ *understand the purpose of library classification systems*

RESPONSES:	1	%	2	%	3	%	4	%	5	%	Om.	%	Mean
School	4	5	14	17	17	21	16	20	28	35	2	2	3.63
Academic	6	16	8	21	11	29	6	16	4	11	2	5	2.83
Public	5	17	6	21	8	28	3	10	7	24	0	0	3.03
Special	0	0	1	17	2	33	2	33	(2 rankings other than 1–5)				3.20
TOTAL	15	10	30	19	28	25	27	17	39	25	4	3	3.30

_____ *correctly locate the women's/men's restroom*

RESPONSES:	1	%	2	%	3	%	4	%	5	%	Om.	%	Mean
School	26	32	4	5	5	6	1	1	23	28	22	27	2.85
Academic	15	39	3	8	1	3	1	3	9	24	8	21	2.52
Public	9	30	2	7	3	10	2	7	7	24	6	21	2.83
Special	5	83	0	0	1	17	0	0	0	0	0		1.33
TOTAL	56	36	9	9	10	6	4	3	39	25	36	23	2.67

_____ properly recognize and use microforms

RESPONSES:	1	%	2	%	3	%	4	%	5	%	Om.	%	Mean
School	8	10	8	10	25	31	14	17	14	17	12	15	3.26
Academic	6	16	7	18	9	24	7	18	5	13	4	11	2.94
Public	8	28	9	31	8	28	1	3	1	3	2	7	2.19
Special	1	17	1	17	3	50	1	17	0	0	0	0	2.67
TOTAL	23	15	15	16	45	29	24	15	20	13	18	12	2.95

_____ effectively use common reference tools such as almanacs,
atlases, dictionaries, and encyclopedias

RESPONSES:	1	%	2	%	3	%	4	%	5	%	Om.	%	Mean
School	1	1	1	1	11	14	12	15	54	67	2	2	4.48
Academic	1	3	2	5	10	26	12	32	13	34	0	0	3.89
Public	0	0	1	3	10	34	9	31	9	31	0	0	3.90
Special	0	0	2	33	1	17	1	17	2	33	0	0	3.50
TOTAL	2	1	5	4	32	21	35	23	78	50	2	1	4.18

17. Do you favor the development of a comprehensive set of standards for library instruction for all types of libraries?

RESPONSES:	YES	%	NO	%	OMITTED	%
School	65	80	15	19	1	1
Academic	29	76	2	5	6	16
Public	19	66	9	31	1	3
Special	3	50	2	33	1	17
TOTAL	116	76	28	18	9	6

RANKING OF SKILLS BY TYPE OF LIBRARY

SCHOOL LIBRARIANS

RANK	SCORE	SKILL
1	4.84	Effectively use the card catalog
2	4.48	Effectively use common reference tools
3	4.40	Correctly use a periodical index & interpret citations
4	4.06	Same
5	3.63	Same
6	3.26	Same
7	2.85	Same

ACADEMIC LIBRARIANS

RANK	SCORE	SKILL
1	4.42	Same
2	4.35	Same
3	3.89	Same
4	3.63	Same
5	2.94	Properly recognize and use microforms
6	2.83	Understand the purpose of library classification systems
7	2.67	Same

PUBLIC LIBRARIANS

RANK	SCORE	SKILL
1	4.79	Same
2	3.90	Effectively use common reference tools
3	3.86	Correctly use a periodical index & interpret the citation
4	3.64	Same
5	3.03	Same
6	2.83	Correctly locate the men's/women's restroom
7	2.19	Properly recognize and use microforms

SPECIAL LIBRARIANS

RANK	SCORE	SKILL
1	4.83	Same
2	3.84	Effectively articulate a reference question to a librarian
3	3.67	Correctly use a periodical index & interpret the citation
4	3.50	Effectively use common reference tools
5	3.20	Same
6	2.67	Same
7	1.33	Same

AL "SCARFACE" CAPONE:
A SEARCH STRATEGY

James Hart
Southeast Missouri State University

This presentation was developed as part of a course-integrated bibliographic instruction program at Southeast Missouri State University which was modeled after the program at Earlham College. In our program we gave students two hours of library use instruction. During the first hour the students were given a tour of the library and some basic instruction in the use of the card catalog and periodical indexes. The second hour was used to present a search strategy lecture in the classroom. In the classroom it is illustrated by transparencies shown on an overhead projector. In the text below the illustrations are reproduced as near the relevant passages as possible. It was first created for a section of English 150 entitled "'The Jazz Age." Most, but not all students in this class, were freshmen. At the time this presentation was created, student apathy was a major concern. The teacher of "The Jazz Age" specifically requested that a criminal figure be used as an example for the search strategy. I selected Al Capone as being representative of that era. When I came across the article on Capone in Jay Robert Nash's book, *Bloodletters and Badmen*, I felt I had found a subject about whom there would be enough colorful anecdotes to keep a class of young adults interested. I shall now deliver the lecture to you just a I do to the freshmen at Southeast. The presentation begins with this reading from the beginning of Nash's article:

"All of the doors of the Hawthorn Hotel in Cicero, Ill., were barred . . . . Inside, at a long table in the private dining room, dozens of swarthy men in tight tuxedos gulped blood-red wine and devoured linguine coated with shrimp sauce. Al "Scarface" Capone sat smiling at the head of the table.

"At the other end of the table sat three equally happy men — John Scalise, Albert Anselmi, and Joseph 'Hop Toad' Giunta. These men were Big Al's ace gunners, a trio of cold-eyed killers who had . . . mercilessly chopped down rival gangsters and balking politicians by the scores. Scarface was grateful.

109

" 'Saluto, Joe,' Capone said to Guinta and raised his brimming glass of chianti.

" 'Saluto, Scalise, saluto, Anselmi!' . . .

"Al was such a wonderful guy . . . .

"Capone pushed back from the table and got up leisurely, still smiling.

" 'If it wasn't for these three fine boys, where would I be, I ask you?' Capone held onto his smile but his stare was like ice as he took in the now frozen band of gangsters. 'Yes, where would I be?' . . .

" 'I'll tell you where I would be,' Capone said softly. And then he screamed, 'I would be safe from a bullet in the head!' . . .

"He reached beneath the banquet table and withdrew a baseball bat and then raced around the table behind his now petrified three guests.

" 'Bastards! You were gonna get me killed and take over, huh? Bastards!'

"Crash, the bat came down on Joe Giunta's head, crushing his skull and killing him instantly. He moved over to Scalise next and slammed the ballbat down to cave in his head also. Eyes begging and lips bitten so hard the blood ran down his chin, Albert Anselmi took the same death blow looking straight ahead.

"Capone's eyes bulged and his porcine, florid face glistened with sweat. He breathed heavily, hushed swearwords gushing from his mouth like spittle . . . . 'Get 'em outa here!' he roared and several men scrambled to remove the bodies.

"This was a typical Capone dinner in Chicago, May 7, 1929 . . . .

"In the space of a dozen bullet-torn years he rose from an obscure bouncer in Big Jim Colsimo's posh restaurant on Wabash Avenue, to the total blood-drenched ruler of Chicago. By then he was only thirty years old and he made $5,000,000 a year." (Nash, pp. 97--98.)

As you can tell from the passage that I just read you from Jay Robert Nash's *Bloodletters and Badmen*, the subject of my talk is Al Capone, possibly the most infamous criminal of all time.[1] I selected this subject for two reasons: first, because I think it is typical of the subjects you will be writing on and second, because it illustrates the ideas about library research that I want to get across to you. I did the research on this subject as if I were going to do a paper

---

[1] Except for the introduction, which was prepared in advance, and the passage from Nash's book, this talk was delivered at LOEX without a prepared text but with the aid of notes. The text from this point on is an edited conflation of transcripts of recordings of several versions. In most classes it was delivered from memory.

on it. Of course, I'm not going to do the paper. Now I will describe to you what I did in the library when I did my research.

The first place I went for information on Capone was the general encyclopedias, the *Americana* and the *Britannica*. I found that they had short, dictionary-like articles that gave date of birth, date of death, a short explanation of why Capone was famous but no bibliographic references. These were good introductory articles, but they were certainly not sufficient to base a paper on, so I went to the *Dictionary of American History*.

Now you may be asking yourselves, "How did he know about the *Dictionary of American History*?" The answer is really very simple. I know because librarians are trained to know these kinds of things. And you can take advantage of our knowledge by going to the reference desk and telling me or any of my colleagues about any problems you may be having with your research.

The *Dictionary of American History* had an article entitled "Crime, Organized," that attempted to cover the history of organized crime in the United States from the very beginning to the middle of the twentieth century. The article was four pages long, and it had a bibliography that listed ten books, four of which seemed as if they might be useful for my purposes. As we will find out later, one of them was.

Now I've just mentioned the term bibliography. Can anybody tell me what a bibliography is? . . . (At this point I look to the audience for a response. There is usually one student in each class who at least has a vague idea of what a bibliography is.) A bibliography is a list of writings on a particular subject or by a particular author arranged in a useful way. A bibliography can list all kinds of writings: books, periodical articles, government documents, pamphlets or any other type. For your purposes a bibliography is a list of the books, articles or whatever else you may read to get information for your paper. The works that are listed in the bibliography at the end of the article in the *Dictionary of American History* are the ones that the author of the article read to get information for it. A bibliography can be arranged in various ways: alphabetically by authors' names, chronologically, or geographically. A bibliography can be comprehensive or selective. A comprehensive bibliography attempts to list everything ever published from the beginning of time to the present from anywhere in the world on a particular subject. A selective bibliography selects certain items from that comprehensive bibliography according to some principle, for example, someone might compile a selective bibliography of everything written on Al Capone in the English language from 1930 to 1950. Now the bibliography in the *Dictionary of American History* was a selective bibliography arranged alphabetically by authors' last names.

Next I went to Jay Robert Nash's *Bloodletters and Badmen*. I found out about this book the same way I found out about the *Dictionary of American History*; that is to say I already knew about it because I am a reference librarian. This had a seven-page article on Capone, a three-page article on his gang, and a six-page article on Johnny Torrio. Johnny Torrio was a particularly important person in Al Capone's life. Can anybody tell us who Torrio was? Does anybody know anything about him? (No one has responded to this question yet.) Torrio was a friend of Capone's when they were growing up in Hell's Kitchen. He is the one who first asked Capone to come to Chicago. He turned all of his holdings over to Capone when he retired for the first time in 1925. At that time he was worth between twenty and thirty million dollars. Asbury says that at one time " . . . Torrio commanded the services of between seven and eight hundred gunmen . . . . " (Asbury, p. 325.) He was rather unusual for a gangster. He never smoked or drank, he loved classical music, and he liked to spend his evenings at home with his wife. Asbury says, "As an organizer and administrator of underworld affairs Johnny Torrio is unsurpassed in the annals of American crime; he was probably the nearest thing to a real master mind that this country has yet produced." (Asbury, pp. 320–21.) The bibliography in *Bloodletters and Badmen* was very long, and the text had no references or footnotes to refer me to any particular items in that bibliography, so I decided not to use it. In addition, Albini's *American Mafia*, which was the one work we have from the bibliography in the *Dictionary of American History*, turned out to be the key that I needed, and that is the work I shall talk about next.

I looked up Albini's book in the card catalog and brought it down from the stacks. I approached this work by looking "Capone, Alphonse" up in the index. It referred me to certain passages in the book concerning Capone. Now sometimes these passages would be embedded in a paragraph, a page, or a chapter that was about Capone or his operations. I read these paragraphs, or pages, or chapters to get information for my paper. As I read those sections, I looked for footnotes. The footnotes led me to references at the end of each chapter. Those references listed other books and articles that had more information on Capone. These are the books and articles that Albini used to get information for his book. (At this point I turn to the illustrations, say something such as "I took note of the following references," and point to each reference in the illustration as I read it aloud.)

Next I located each of these works in the library and examined them. I looked the books up in the card catalog, and I looked the periodical title up in the "List of Periodicals in Kent Library." This is a part of the process of doing research. When you find a book, examine it as I examined Albini's book. Follow up the footnotes and note down references from the bibliography. Locate those items and repeat the process. Keep going until you have a good enough list of material from which to write a paper.

The first item listed in Albini's bibliography is Asbury's *Gem of the Prairie*. This book devoted the last fifty-five pages to the period from the rise of Johnny Torrio to Capone's arrest on October 6, 1931, for income tax evasion. *Gem of the Prairie* had thirty-four references in the index to passages concerning Capone. I looked up the footnotes in the bibliography, which referred me to . . . (at this point I turn to the illustration and point to each reference as I read it aloud) Bennett's *Chicago Gangland*, etc.

The next work listed in Albini's bibliography was Pasley's *Al Capone*. Now this has two unusual features. First, it has no bibliography or footnotes, and second, it was published in 1930. Can anybody tell us why these are unusual features? (The few students who have a vague idea of the significance of these features usually make the point that Capone was still alive and operating at the time.) Let me try to get this idea across to you by asking you a few questions. If you meet a friend of yours on the street, and he tells you a story, and you ask him who told him the story, and he says, "Oh, sorry, can't tell you," aren't you a little suspicious about who his source is? Don't you want to know whether his source was a good authority or not? Well, isn't the same thing true of a book? If it doesn't have a bibliography, you can't tell what the author's sources were. Well, that was my reaction when I first picked up Pasley's book. Now it's possible, just possible, that Pasley talked to Capone. And Capone might have lied to him. After all, why would a murderer hesitate to lie? And Capone was well known for his publicity stunts, he loved to see his name in the newspaper. On the other hand, if Pasley talked to him, Capone could have told the truth. If this is the case, then Pasley may have some information that no one else has, so I would recommend that you use this book cautiously. Keep this in mind because we'll get back to this question a little later on.

Going on down Albini's bibliography, we come to Peterson's works next. In contrast to Pasley's book, we can be pretty sure Peterson's works are reliable. I can say that because there was a blurb on the first page of his article that told what his qualifications were. At the time the article was published, he was the Operating Director of the Chicago Crime Commission. He worked for the F.B.I. from 1930 to 1942 and was successively head of their offices in Milwaukee, St. Louis, and Boston. He was a member of the Illinois Bar and had an earned J.D. degree and an honorary Doctorate of Laws. So he not only had academic experience, but he also had practical experience fighting crime. So, where there is a contradiction between what Peterson says and what some other writer says, I'm going to tend to believe Peterson.

Then I looked at *Barbarians in Our Midst* a little more closely. I looked in the index, and it had thirty-eight references to passages concerning Capone. Most of them led me to chapter seven. So I read chapter seven, and I followed up the footnotes to the notes at the end of the chapter. It has no separate bibliography at the end of the book. Those notes listed not only books, but also newspaper and magazine articles. (At this point I turn to the illustration, say something such as "I took note of the following references," and point to each reference in the illustration as I read it aloud.) I then looked at "Shades of Capone," Peterson's periodical article, and I found that it summarized the Capone era of crime in Chicago merely as a prelude to a fuller discussion of crime in the forties and fifties. I read that part of it that summarized the Capone era and found that it gave a little information that I found nowhere else.

Now as I went through the items listed in Albini's bibliography I read the parts that seemed relevant. As I read more and more, I got a clearer idea of what kind of paper I could write, if I were going to write one. The more I knew, the easier it was to break my subject down into subtopics.

The last item listed in Albini's bibliography was Wendt and Kogan's *Lords of the Levy*. I had a little trouble in locating it. Albini cites it as *Lords of the Levy*, but that wasn't in the title catalog, so I looked in the author catalog under Lloyd Wendt. I found another book listed called *Bosses in Lusty Chicago*. I thought it was just possible that Wendt and Kogan might have done a lot of research, turned out *Lords of the Levy* and decided that they had some extra information left over; so they wrote another book on the same subject. So I went upstairs and got it in the hopes that it might help me. When I examined it, I looked on the back of the title page. It said that *Bosses in Lusty Chicago* had formerly been published as *Lords of the Levy*.

Has anybody ever heard of the Levy area in Chicago? (No one has responded to this question yet.) I had never heard of it before I did this research, and the research never did clear up for me exactly what it was. My impression is that it was a segregated area in which vice was allowed to flourish as long as it didn't spread into other areas of the city. It was located between Wabash Avenue and the south branch of the Chicago River, and it extended south of Adams Street for about a mile. It was filled with saloons, gambling houses, and brothels, and it was dominated politically from the 1890s to the 1940s by "Bathhouse" John Coughlin and "Hinky Dink" Kenna. "Bathhouse" John represented this area in city hall off and on during the whole fifty-year period. As their influence declined,

Capone's rose. In fact, near the end, they were on Capone's payroll.

Capone had a lot of men on his payroll. This was what allowed his organization to operate for such a long time with such a small amount of trouble. He paid protection money to policemen, high police officials, city councilmen and judges. It was important to him to make sure that corruptible officials were elected to office. He not only paid them, but he also guaranteed them success at the polls. At that time, it was not unusual that on an election day men were killed, voters were kidnapped, the polls were raided, and ballots were taken from voters who were just about to drop them in the ballot box. It was estimated that Johnny Torrio paid about $400,000 per year in protection money, and it was known by word of mouth that Torrio had established a pay off station at a very public place in downtown Chicago. (Asbury, p. 337.)

Lords of the Levy devotes the last chapter to Capone's rise to power, and the bibliography lists these items: (at this point I turn to the illustration and point to each reference as I read it aloud) Asbury's *Gem of the Prairie*, etc.

You may have noticed that certain works have been referred to over and over again. For example, Pasley's *Al Capone* has been referred to four times. When you do your research and go through bibliography after bibliography, you can expect to find certain authors and certain works cited again and again. These are the works that most authors in the field agree should be read even if you don't agree with some of the ideas in them, and these are the first ones you should search for when you do your research.

I've got a pretty good list of books now, and I've got one reference to a periodical article. Now I need to get more references to periodical articles and some newspaper articles, if I can find them.

Since my subject was biographical, the first place I went was to *Biography Index*. I looked in it from 1952 to the present, and I found references to these two articles: (at this point I turn to the illustration and point to each reference as I read it aloud) Mitchell's "Said Chicago's Al Capone: I Give the Public What the Public Wants . . . ," etc.

Next I went to the *Humanities Index*. I looked through it from 1974 through 1980, that is for six years. I found no references whatsoever to anything remotely related to Al Capone, so I concluded that it wasn't worth my while to look any further in the *Humanities Index*. Now this doesn't mean that I shouldn't have looked there though. I have constructed a search strategy, a plan for doing my research in the library. I cannot know beforehand which indexes will or will not list articles on my subject. I can only look at those works which I think will probably have some references that I can use. I only know from hindsight which ones do and which ones don't. But you can't construct a search strategy from hindsight. You've got to look at everything that might possibly prove to be useful and that means you've got to look at some things that won't prove to be useful.

After that I went to the *Readers' Guide* for the years 1925 through 1937. I found references to a total of twenty articles, quite a few really. I've copied only four of them here, and I want to draw your attention to the second one. (At this point I turn to the illustration, point to the relevant reference and read it aloud.) I read the review, and it said that Pasley's book contains a lot of material that appears nowhere else and that it was written by a Chicago newspaperman who was well suited to write the book. So I found out that Pasley's book is a good, reliable book. It may, in fact, turn out to be one of my major sources.

The last place I went was to the *Index to the New York Times* for the years 1927 through 1933. I found a great number of references to newspaper articles there. In the year 1927 I found no references; in the year 1928 I found a full column of references; in 1929 another full column; in 1930 a column and a half; in 1931 three full columns of references; in 1932 one column; and in 1933 I found fourteen references to articles about Capone.

Now, newspapers differ from magazines and books. Newspapers give you the most recent news. They tell you what's happening right now. They will report a broken series of isolated incidents, not a continuous story line. A periodical article and a book will give you, a book even more so than a periodical article, more depth and a wider perspective than a newspaper story, so I'm going to use newspaper stories to highlight a certain selected incident. The incident I have selected is the St. Valentine's Day Massacre. Now I'm sure almost everybody has heard of that. Can anybody fill us in and tell us any more about it? (No one has responded to this question yet.) The St. Valentine's Day Massacre occurred on February 14, 1929. Five of Capone's men, three dressed in police uniforms and two in street clothes, pulled up in a large sedan to Bugs Moran's headquarters at 2122 N. Clark. Now Moran was the head of the rival Northside gang of Irishmen. They made most of their money from gambling and holding up Capone's beer trucks now and then, but they didn't engage in any prostitution at all, which is how Capone and Torrio really got started. Before the Volstead Act was passed, Capone and Torrio made most of their money from prostitution. The Northside Irishmen, on the other hand, were upstanding young men and would never engage in something so dirty. At the time that Capone's men drove up to Bugs Moran's garage, there were only seven men in it. The three Capone men in police uniform lined Moran's men up on one side of the garage and disarmed them. The men in plain clothes stepped forward and machine-gunned them. One of those men was not a member of Moran's gang. He was an optometrist who liked hanging around with gangsters in his spare time. Joe Giunta, John Scalise and Jack McGurn were arrested for the murders. McGurn proved that he was doing something else at the time, and Scalise and Anselmi were killed before the trial.

The *Times Index* had a full column of references that went from February 15 to March 24 about the killings. I have copied only a few of those references down here. If you look at what I've copied down, I think you get a pretty good idea of the story: (at this point I turn to the illustration as I read it aloud). I want to draw your attention to this last item here, " . . . witness in Moran gang killings, is kidnapped then released in Detroit; witnesses fail to appear." This was the common run of things at that time. Witnesses just wouldn't show up. They feared that if they testified against Capone or any of his men that they'd be killed. And if they weren't killed, it wouldn't do any good to testify because very likely the judge was on Capone's payroll. And if the judge wasn't, then Capone would probably bribe the jury. And even if the judge and the jury were straight, and they got a conviction, it was likely the criminal would be pardoned by the governor. Look at this (here I point to the relevant reference). "G. Moran says he does not know who the murderers are." At the time that Capone's men pulled up to the garage, Moran was coming up the alley next to the garage, and, when he saw these men get out of the sedan in police uniforms, he went the other way. He didn't care whether they were policemen or Capone's men. He didn't want to talk to either of them. He went into hiding for several days. (Here I point to the relevant reference.) The next reference mentions that Capone was questioned at Miami, Florida on the sixteenth. Capone planned the St. Valentine's Day Massacre in Chicago, and then he had gone down to Miami Beach. He had bought a large mansion there, but the people of Florida didn't want him living there. So the district attorney wanted to talk to him. So he went down to Florida, made an appointment to talk to the district attorney; and then just before he went to the appointment, called Chicago and arranged for the St. Valentine's Day Massacre. At the very moment that the guns were firing in Chicago, Capone was talking to the district attorney in Miami Beach.

Let me summarize the strategy that I have used to do my research. I started out with the lowest level of sources, the introductory sources that give a little bit of information and only a few or even no bibliographic references, the general encyclopedias. Then I went to the intermediate level sources, the *Dictionary of American History* in this case. It had a nice little bibliography that referred me to an advanced source, Albini's *American Mafia*. And that referred me to Asbury's *Gem of the Prairie*, Peterson's *Barbarians in Our Midst*, Pasley's *Al Capone*, and Wendt and Kogan's *Lords of the Levy*. Asbury's *Gem of the Prairie* then led me to Bennett's *Chicago Gangland*, Landesco's *Organized Crime in Chicago*, and Reckless's *Vice in Chicago*. I then checked the *Biography Index*, the *Humanities Index*, the *Readers' Guide* and the *Index to the New York Times* for references to periodical and newspaper articles.

Research is not a matter of luck. If you choose a topic on which our library has enough information for you to write a paper, and you plan your research in advance, you should have at least as much success as I had.

WARNING:

WHAT YOU ARE ABOUT TO
WITNESS MAY NOT BE SUITABLE
FOR CHILDREN

PARENTAL GUIDANCE IS SUGGESTED

AL "Scarface" CAPONE:
A SEARCH STRATEGY

I

The Encyclopedia Americana. New York: Americana, 1980.

II

The New Encyclopedia Britannica. 15th ed. Chicago: Encyclopaedia Britannica, 1974.

III

Dictionary of American History. Rev. ed. New York: Scribner, 1976–78.

Article: Crime, Organized.

Relevant bibliographic reference:

> Albini, Joseph L. *The American Mafia: Genesis of a Legend.* New York: Appleton-Century-Crofts, 1971.

> A bibliography is a list of writings on a particular subject or author arranged in a useful way.

IV

Nash, Jay Robert. *Bloodletters and Badmen: A Narrative Encyclopedia of American Criminals from the Pilgrims to the Present.* New York: M. Evans, 1973.

V

Albini, Joseph L. *The American Mafia: Genesis of a Legend.* New York: Appleton-Century-Crofts, 1971.

Relevant bibliographic references:

Asbury, Herbert. *Gem of the Prairie: An Informal History of the Chicago Underworld.* New York: Knoft, 1940.

Pasley, Fred D. *Al Capone: The Biography of a Self-Made Man.* n.p.: Ives Washburn, 1930.

Peterson, Virgil W. *Barbarians in Our Midst: A History of Chicago Crime and Politics.* Boston: Little, Brown, 1952.

Peterson, Virgil W. "Shades of Capone." *The Annals.* CCCXLVII (May 1963), 30–39.

Wendt, Lloyd and Kogan, Herman. *Lords of the Levee: The Story of Bathhouse John and Hinky Dink.* Indianapolis: Bobbs-Merrill, 1943.

VI

Asbury, Herbert. *Gem of the Prairie: An Informal History of the Chicago Underworld.* New York: Knopf, 1940.

Relevant bibliographic references:

Bennett, James O'Donnell. *Chicago Gang Land: The True Story of Chicago Crime.* Chicago: Chicago Tribune, 1929.

Landesco, John. "Organized Crime in Chicago," Part III *Illinois Crime Survey.* Chicago: n.p. 1929.

Pasley, Fred D. *Al Capone: The Biography of a Self-Made Man.* New York: Ives Washburn, 1930.

Reckless, Walter C. *Vice in Chicago.* Chicago: University of Chicago Press, 1933.

VII

Pasley, Fred D. *Al Capone: The Biography of a Self-Made Man*. New York: Ives Washburn, 1930.

VIII

Peterson, Virgil. *Barbarians in Our Midst: A History of Chicago Crime and Politics*. Boston: Little, Brown, 1952.

Peterson, Virgil. "Shades of Capone." *The Annals*. CCCXLVII, (May 1963), 30–39.

Relevant bibliographic references:

Asbury, Herbert. *Gem of the Prairie: An Informal History of the Chicago Underworld*. New York: A.A. Knopf, 1940.

Landesco, John. "Organized Crime in Chicago," Part III *Illinois Crime Survey*. Chicago: n.p. 1929.

Pasley, Fred D. *Al Capone: The Biography of a Self-Made Man*. New York: Ives Washburn, 1930.

Wendt, Lloyd and Kogan, Herman. *Lords of the Levee: The Story of Bathhouse John and Hinky Dink*. Indianapolis: Bobbs-Merrill, 1943.

IX

Wendt, Lloyd and Kogan, Herman. *Bosses in Lusty Chicago: The Story of Bathhouse John and Hinky Dink*. Bloomington: Indiana University Press, 1967.

Relevant bibliographic references:

Asbury, Herbert. *Gem of the Prairie: An Informal History of the Chicago Underworld*. New York: A.A. Knopf, 1940.

Bennett, James O'Donnell. *Chicago Gang Land: The True Story of Chicago Crime*. Chicago: Chicago Tribune, 1929.

Landesco, John. "Organized Crime in Chicago," Part III *Illinois*

Crime Survey. Chicago: n.p. 1929.

Pasley, Fred D. *Al Capone: The Biography of a Self-Made Man.* New York: Ives Washburn, 1930.

Reckless, Walter C. *Vice in Chicago*. Chicago: University of Chicago Press, 1933.

X

Biography Index 1952/55 through 1980.

Subject heading: Capone, Alphonse.

References:

Mitchell, J.G. "Said Chicago's Al Capone: I Give the Public What the Public Wants . . . " *Am Heritage* 30:82–93 F '79.

Sullivan, T. and Kobler, J. "Caddying for a Man Who Never Shot Par," *Sports Illus*. 37:73-8+ N 6 72.

XI

Humanities Index 1974--1980.

XII

Readers' Guide 1925--1932.

Subject heading: Capone, Alphonse.

Selected references:

Al Capone's victory. *New Repub* 67:167 J1 1 '31

Czar of Chicago: review of *Al Capone: biography of a self-made man*, by F.D. Palsey. W.R. Burnett. *Sat R Lit* 7:240 0 18 '30

Jessica and Al Capone. K.F. Gerould. *Harper* 163:93--7 Je '31

Rise of a racketeer. L.W. Hunt. pors *Outlook* 156:574-6+ D 10 '30

XIII

Index to the New York Times 1927--1933

Subject headings: Capone, Alphonse
                            Crime and Criminals--
                            Illinois

Selected references:

7 gangsters slain by firing squad of rivals; G Moran leader of wiped out gang, missing; some of executioners in police uniform; A Capone sought, F 15, 1:8

A Capone questioned at Miami, Fla, with reference to Chicago killings, F 16, 14:8

G Moran says he does not know who murderes are, F 17, 24:4

L W Tacker, witness in Moran gang killings, is kidnapped then released in Detroit; witnesses fail to appear, F 24, 3:1

WHAT YOU HAVE JUST WITNESSED/
IS BASED ON A TRUE STORY
SOME OF THE FACTS HAVE/
BEEN SUBJECTED TO LITERARY LICENSE

THE NAMES HAVE BEEN CHANGED
TO PROTECT THE INNOCENT

THE WORLD AND 37.4 CANDY BARS; OR
THE SCHOOL LIBRARY MEDIA CENTER AND
CURRICULUM INVOLVEMENT

Lyle E. Grooters
St. Clair County Community College

"The World and 37.4 Candy Bars" is a curriculum simulation project that is always stimulating! Les Standwood devised the game as a powerful method of presenting the concepts of overpopulation, starvation, and deprivation to his high school students. His article appeared in *Media & Methods*, September, 1979.[1] I have adapted this simulation to library instruction, and find it packs an equally impressive wallop! Getting students interested in and excited about doing research is not always an easy task. An unusual approach may provide the light at the end of the tunnel, and be the desired catalyst.

One of the most important goals in library media skills instruction is to integrate media skills with all curriculum areas. It is essential that this responsibility be shared by both the classroom teacher and the librarian. The research or term paper assignment provides an excellent opportunity for the teacher and librarian to work as a team to whet the appetite of the student for doing the research and for providing the tools with which to do it.

Let's start by going back to the beginning. How do we learn? We learn through our senses: through taste, touch, smell, hearing; and not surprisingly, the greatest percentage of learning is through sight.

WE LEARN:

1%	Through Taste
1½%	Through Touch
3½%	Through Smell
11%	Through Hearing
83%	Through Sight

Chart 1. Learning through the senses.[2]

Let's consider how long we retain this information. Researchers say we remember about 10 percent of what we read, 20 percent of what we hear, 30 percent of what we see, and 50 percent of what we see and hear. But, it is estimated that 70 percent of what people say as they talk is retained. Thus, even greater retention is achieved when seeing, hearing, and discussion are combined. In addition, physical involvement can increase retention to 90 percent.[2]

One more consideration is recall of information. We'll divide this into two categories: three hours later, and three days later.

METHODS OF INSTRUCTION	RECALL 3 HOURS LATER	RECALL 3 DAYS LATER
A. Telling when used alone	70%	10%
B. Showing when used alone	72%	20%
C. When a blend of telling and showing is used	85%	65%

Chart 2. Effect of visualization on delayed recall.[2]

Obviously, involvement and participation are key factors in retention.

With these facts in mind, my immediate goal is to get *you* involved and concerned with overpopulation, starvation and deprivation; as you, in turn, will hope to motivate your students. Would telling you that in 1800 the world population was one billion, and that it increased to two billion by 1930 impress you? By 1950, only 20 years later, our world had mushroomed to three billion persons. Overwhelming! But, are the numbers meaningful? Showing you this transparency might help your recollection of facts, but a different approach might be even more effective. Let's get this world population down to a size with which we can relate. If the world were a global village of 100 people, 70 would be unable to read, only one would have a college education, over 50 would be suffering from malnutrition, 80 would be living in what we call substandard housing. Six would be Americans, and these same six would have half the village's wealth, while the rest of the 94 people would exist on the other half.[3] Conceivable numbers paint a more meaningful picture; but to really drive home the concept of overpopulation and world resources, we will play the game, "The World and 37.5 Candy Bars."

Preplanning for the game when it is used with students could involve introduction of a term paper project by the classroom teacher. Then, 40 volunteers are chosen to bring a common sized candy bar to class the next day (or the bars may be provided by the presenter), and to take part in the game. The 40 students represent the world population, the candy bars the world gross national product or food supply. The world area is represented by a space 24 by 20 feet marked on the floor in the manner indicated by Chart 3. Forty cards with the names of world areas in the proportion indicated on Chart 4, are placed face down in a box to be drawn at random by the volunteers.

Candy bars are deposited in a central location on the day of the game. Draw a card, and proceed to the proper area. Each group should choose a leader who will distribute the "food supply" allocated to that area. Refer to Chart 4. It is not easy to divide five candy bars among 24 people in Asia, and watch six Americans receive 5½ candy bars each. The disproportionate distribution of land and goods becomes painfully obvious, and should be a good basis for thought and discussion. It should become clear that the game has provided some startling information, but that there is much more that can be discovered by looking in the right places!

Enter the card catalog! After the research topic has been selected, the logical place to start is the card catalog. I have three examples on population from our card catalog: a book, a filmstrip and a cassette tape. By placing these entries on overhead transparencies, a review can be made of the different parts of the catalog card, such as the call number, type of media, subject heading, etc. Mention the "see" and "see also" references. In this example we are referred to the subject headings "food supply" and "birth control." There also may be a reference in your card catalog to consult the vertical file for additional information.

Reference materials, such as encyclopedias, almanacs, maps, and statistical abstracts should not be overlooked as sources for term paper research. The encyclopedias have been a popular source of information since elementary school. They will usually give an overview or summary of the subject that is being researched. On these transparencies are a few examples of statistics on "World Population" that were obtained from almanacs, statistical abstracts, and even the *Guinness Book of World Records*. The latter states that the African country of Niger Republic has the highest birth rate, 52.2 per thousand. What country do you suppose has the lowest? The Vatican does, with zero!

Another good reference source for information is the newspaper.

At SCCCC, we receive the *New York Times* along with the *Index*. This next transparency shows a few examples of the topic "Birth Control." There is a short summary of each article along with a reference notation stating the date, page, and column number of the issue in which the article appeared. All of our issues of the *New York Times* over a year old are on microfilm. This exercise provides a good opportunity to teach and/or review the use of microfilm and microfiche machines.

So far we have covered the use of the card catalog, reference sources, and newspapers. That leaves journals and magazines, along with the various related indexes. Here is a wealth of information, but finding it can be difficult unless students are instructed in the use of the periodical indexes. Most high schools have *Readers' Guide to Periodical Literature*. Once again we will use the subjects of overpopulation, birth control, and world food supply to demonstrate the correct procedures in using this index and the steps in actually locating these materials.

This next transparency refers to an article on overpopulation:

Profile of a world overflowing with people. il *U.S. News* 82:54-5 Mr 28 '77[4]

At this point, a review of the meanings of the various abbreviations and figures is appropriate. Secondly, establish whether this particular issue of *U.S. News and World Report* is available. Finally, comes the explanation of the check out policy in the library concerning magazines and journals.

The next few transparencies are examples on the same subjects, but use the *Educational Index* and *Social Science Index*. There will be a number of magazines and journals to which your library does not subscribe. Perhaps these items may be available in the public library or a nearby college library. In some cases interlibrary loan is a possibility. The next transparency shows the information that is required before we can send for an article. It is important that the students know how long it takes before they can expect the article. In our case, it usually takes ten to fourteen days, which would be too late for those whose term paper is due in two days.

This transparency will conclude this part of my presentation. It seems appropriate to the topic of world hunger:

If you give a man a fish, you have fed him for a day;

If you teach him how to fish, you have fed him for a lifetime.

Next, I would like to acquaint you with a very useful publication called *The Wisconsin Library Media Skills Guide*.[5]

This 200 page guide contains:
* 17 basic skills organized in 5 broad areas
  ---- orientation
  ---- organization and utilization of resources

   --- selection of resources
   --- research and study skills
   --- production and utilization of materials
* Overview in chart form of the levels of instruction for each skill at each grade level
* performance objectives listed grade by grade
* skills treated individually at each grade level including:
   --- student objectives
   --- staff activities
   --- suggested resources
   --- skill evaluation
* annotated bibliographies for grade level groupings: Pre-school--6, 6--9, 9--12.

It was developed by a group of school and college library media specialists. It was my privilege to serve as chairperson and editor of this venture. You should have a brochure in the handout of materials with additional information about the guide. I also have a copy available for you to look at after this presentation.

I would like to conclude by showing you *The Periodical Index*, a sound/slide program we use in our library instruction program at SCCCC. The others are *LRC Orientation* and *The Card Catalog*. All beginning English students are required to view these three programs, and complete a two-page worksheet, which is graded, and becomes a part of their final grade in the English course.

It is my hope that seeing, hearing, and doing has made this a stimulating 90 minutes. My challenge to you is that you incorporate seeing, hearing, and doing into a meaningful experience for the students *you* serve.

NOTES

1. Stanwood, Les. "The World and 37.4 Candy Bars," *Media & Methods*, (September, 1979).

2. Blair, Glen, M. Jones, R. Steward, and Ray H. Simpson. *Educational Psychology*, 3d ed. New York: MacMillan Co., 1968.

3. Turner, Dale. Included in a sermon on World Problems. University Congregational Church of Seattle, Washington.

4. *Readers' Guide to Periodical Literature*. Vol. 37, p. 882. Population − Overpopulation.

5. *The Wisconsin Library Media Skills Guide*, edited by Lyle E. Grooters. Wisconsin Library Association, (August, 1979).

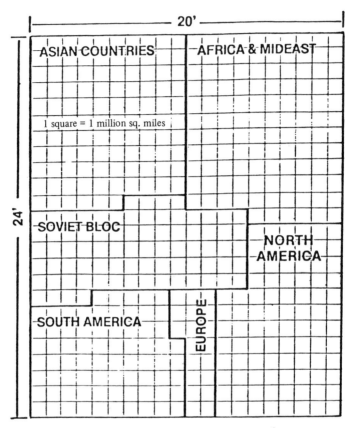

Chart 3. Classroom design.[1]

LAND AREAS	Square Miles (1=1,000,000,000)	Population (1-100,000,000)		Gross Nat'l Product (1=$100,000,000,000)		1977 Petroleum Prod. Consumption (1=1,000,000,000 barrels)
		1975	2000	1975	2000	
Asia	10.6	24	39	5.0	10.0	3.7
Africa & Mideast	11.6	3	8	1.0	1.5	1.1
Soviet Countries	8.6	3	4	5.0	12.0	3.6
South America	7.5	3	6	1.4	3.5	0.9
Europe	1.9	5	5	14.0	22.0	5.0
North America	7.6	2	3	11.0	20.0	7.9
TOTALS	ʼ47.8	40	65	37.4	69.0	22.2

Chart 4. World land areas.[1]

BASIC COLLEGE RESEARCH:
A UNIVERSITY TEACHER'S VIEW

Carol Lee Saffioti
University of Wisconsin–Parkside

Teaching the methods of basic research writing on the university level in a formal course setting has the following positive features: it reinforces the emphasis placed on good working knowledge and use of library sources; it closely ties the concept of the "library as classroom" with that concept of the rather more sacrosanct, traditional classroom; and finally, it provides students with guidance from faculty whose specialty is writing, as students focus attention on the process from formulation of a sound, workable idea, to integration of varying conclusions in the formulation of their own conclusions. Also, the formal class introduces students to the standards applied broadly to most fields of undergraduate-oriented research that they will encounter as they progress through school. Ironically, however, by the very structured orientation of such a course, problems arise as the students focus on instruction, objectives, goals and skills related to the completion of a requirement. In particular, from my point of view as a teacher, I see a major problem as this one: students involved in a research writing course, and with so-called "basic skills" courses generally, are encouraged to externalize rather than internalize their own learning goals, and they show an increasingly disturbing penchant for allowing, and expecting an institution, or a sector of it, to tell them what the limits of their potential as well as their performance may be. Such a premise may not be the expected one from a faculty member such as myself, working for five years to help develop a curriculum, to write and receive grants, and indeed teach the writing course of which I speak, as I address an audience of skilled authorities whose knowledge of the word and its boundaries continues to strike me humbly as I learn from them; for the achievement of libraries in the area of instructional skills development has surpassed that of faculties' in many cases by design, and perhaps even by ability. Nevertheless, the purpose of this discussion will be fourfold: to describe the competence-based program of writing at the University of Wisconsin-Parkside from which the course, The Library Research Paper, has developed; to define in some detail the aspirations

Parkside has had for its students in the area of research gathering and writing; to explain generally the application of the "workbook" approach that librarian Patricia Berge and I have extended from the area of library use into the area of research writing; and most importantly, to suggest that a *teacher's* view of research is more significant than that of an instructor, as I shall use the terms.

Collegiate Skills at UW--Parkside

The Collegiate Skills program at Parkside is the response of a medium sized (approximately 6,000 students) four-year campus of the University of Wisconsin system to its mission to provide college education to students of a multiplicity of ages, as well as work, educational, and cultural backgrounds. As pointed out in a draft of the program in 1976,

> An effective student needs to read, write, speak English, use basic mathematical skills, and be able to utilize library resources. The University is committed to developing tests in these areas, to establishing a variety of programs aimed at helping the student acquire the necessary level of competence, and to requiring that a student meet this standard early in his work at Parkside.[1]

The university thus defined a goal that graduates must demonstrate mastery of skills in the areas of library use as well as the more traditionally defined "basic skills" areas, and within the area of writing, two major areas were specified: rhetorical and research-related writing. Thus, instruction in research writing methods has been separated out from the traditional freshman composition course. Figure 1 identifies the major areas of competency for which placement and proficiency testing instruments have been developed, as well as the levels of courses that would offer preparatory or college level experience. In addition, three levels of competence help identify the abilities of Parkside students from high school or entry level, through to, and including areas of advanced work within a specialization, discipline, or major:

Level I   The level generally thought of as that of a high school graduate with adequate preparation for college freshman work.

Level II   The level generally thought of as that of a college sophomore with adequate preparation for entry into specialized or upper-level courses. The student must show competence at this level during the sophomore year.

FIGURE 1.

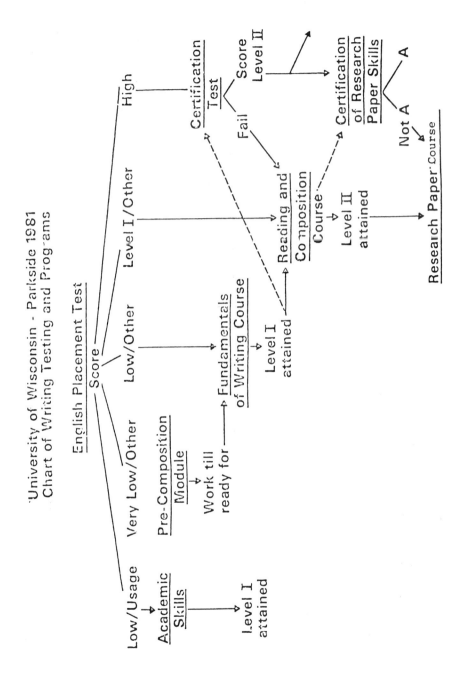

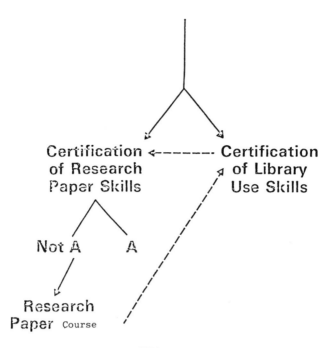

Certification ←------- Certification
of Research   of Library
Paper Skills   Use Skills

Not A   A

Research
Paper Course

FIGURE 2.

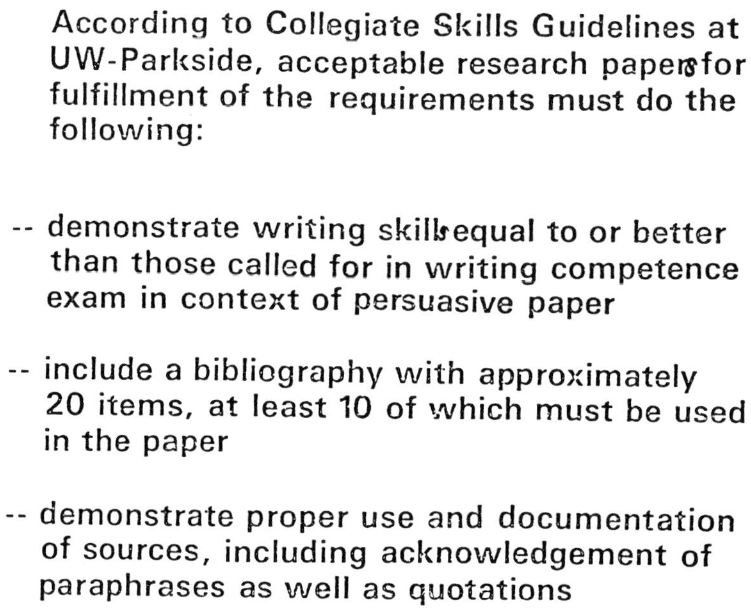

According to Collegiate Skills Guidelines at
UW-Parkside, acceptable research papers for
fulfillment of the requirements must do the
following:

-- demonstrate writing skill equal to or better
   than those called for in writing competence
   exam in context of persuasive paper

-- include a bibliography with approximately
   20 items, at least 10 of which must be used
   in the paper

-- demonstrate proper use and documentation
   of sources, including acknowledgement of
   paraphrases as well as quotations

FIGURE 3.

Level III   The level generally thought of as that of a university graduate; this level will vary considerably, depending upon the student's major field.[2]

Because the program moved swiftly from the planning to the implementation stages in 1977 it was well-noted by the media. In particular, the innovative aspect of the program interesting to teachers of research gathering and writing is the fact that a requirement concerning proficiency in both library use and research writing was, and remains, part of the program.

In order to demonstrate proficiency in library use, students must both complete a self-paced workbook based on the model developed by Miriam Dudley at the University of California, and pass a test developed under the guidance of Carla Stoffle, then assistant director of the Library Learning Center at UW--Parkside. This PSI-based requirement can be completed by most students working approximately ten to twelve hours on the material. The tests are administered in class for students taking the one credit English course (English 102 — the Library Research Paper) and on separate testing dates for others attempting to complete the library use requirement independently (see Figure 2).

In parallel fashion, in order to demonstrate proficiency in research writing, students must submit a paper which satisfies university-established standards (see Figure 3). The paper may be submitted from any research project completed, or it may be generated as the major assignment of English 102. If submitted independent of the formal course, a member, or members, of the English department evaluate its merit. If submitted as part of the course, the English instructor evaluates the student's work, having made other assignments as well. The formal course, considered a Level II course, is one which grants one credit toward university graduation. All of the competence requirements of the Collegiate Skills program at Parkside must be completed by the time students have accumulated 45 credits; if not completed, students face academic probation. Nevertheless, students have several routes to take in order to demonstrate their ability to use the facilities of an academic library to gather research on a topic and to write about it.

The Formal Course Approach

In comparison with other approaches nationally, Parkside does not use the optional or voluntary term paper clinic approach, nor the "mini-course" within composition courses, nor a non-credit modular approach such as that of CCNY reported in *College English*.[3] The English department has accepted the responsibility for administering a course which combines two areas of study that go naturally together: that is, learning to use a library and learning to do research. Thus, the department lends visible support and credibility to the competence program and to the library's efforts in bibliographic instruction. Parkside's approach differs from that at the University of Alabama which does use a PSI format for integrated library instruction but does not cover research writing skills in the same program.[4] Parkside acknowledges the need for formal course instruction in basic research methods and carries this approach forward with content-specific research methods courses later in many majors. Through the use of advanced level III workbooks developed by librarians at Parkside, such courses satisfy that part of the Collegiate Skills program instituted so that students are well qualified to conduct research in their major fields by the time of graduation, when they reach the so-called "level III" competence.[5]

A current directory of library instruction programs in Wisconsin has not been completed; however, if one compares Parkside's approach with those used in Indiana, statewide, one finds the CLUE (Clearinghouse for Library User Education) reported in 1979 that only 13 of 40 academic libraries reported formal courses, and none of these included extensive instruction in actual research writing. Eight of 40 used the clinic approach, and only 18 of 40 required formal library instruction of all graduates.[6] A survey of the California Instructional Improvement Service (CAIS) completed in March of 1981, revealed that for the period 1979–1981, 137 citations for writing program grants were registered in the University of California system; 20 of these were for autotutorial programs, none of which revealed a focus on research writing skills. The workbook approach for mastery of library use developed at the University of California by Miriam Dudley has not yet moved out into the area of instruction in research writing skills.[7] A preliminary survey of library instruction programs described in ERIC document files for the period 1976–1980 reveals no university programs that have integrated a college graduation requirement for both library use and research writing into the curriculum.[8] Yet the problems outlined by Joyce Merriam concerning her survey of high school level instruction persist at the college level as well.[9] And her recommendations can be translated very easily into college level applications:

College students should be tested at time of entry concerning their abilities in library use;

They should receive formal instruction in library use and research writing if they cannot demonstrate competency in these areas within a reasonable time after admission;

Faculty should be encouraged and supported to integrate search strategy into course content, and to integrate library skills into classroom instruction;

English departments should share the responsibility with library staff for instruction in research writing methods at the introductory level;

All departments should take on the responsibility of integrating research writing methods into the curriculum at the advanced level.

At the time of this report, UW--Parkside is embarking on an extensive analysis of the data related to the entire Collegiate Skills program since its inception in 1977. Thus, data presented here are incomplete (see Table I), but the included information gives a general picture of the numbers of students who have completed the library use or the research paper requirement.

How can instructors and faculty work together to help carry out some of these goals emphasized above? One answer, here described, is the formal course. Because Parkside's course in collegiate research skills has been described extensively in the *Wisconsin English Journal* and in *ERIC*, what follows is a description not of the course but of the development and approach of *Basic College Research*, a workbook developed by a librarian and a faculty member working together to make instruction in basic research gathering and writing accessible to all Parkside students.[10]

Basic College Research

Basic College Research is the result of work over the period 1975--1980 to improve the teaching of research writing skills in my freshman classes.[11] The "hand-outs" prepared through various team teaching experiences became unwieldy and it was a fortuitous coincidence that at the time Carla Stoffle and I were considering the preparation of a teacher's manual, Parkside also decided to separate out the research paper from other requirements in the composition course. The manual was prepared through funding which originally came to Parkside as part of an NEH grant for library instruction. While the content--specific workbooks were being prepared, the first version of the introductory level manual was reviewed by Hannelore Rader, then a consultant for the grant. Still unwieldy as a collection of "how-to's" for teachers of English 102, nevertheless the manual was used by several instructors in the 1978--79 year. Major revisions were formulated and completed under support from the University of Wisconsin System Teaching Improvement Grant program in 1980. With twelve chapters, specific objectives for each chapter, a concise text in each chapter, and exercises relevant to each step in the

Table 1

Cumulative Totals–Students Satisfying Competence Requirements in Library Use and Research Writing

As of	Research Paper	Library Skills	
April, 81	711 (P)	1040	(P)
Feb, 81	700	881	
		77	(F)

Computer Dump: records of students not attending for 6 semesters

As of	Research Paper	Library Skills	
Oct, 81	596	884	
		78	(F)
May, 79	200	342	
		40	(F)
May, 78	75	76	
		5	(F)
Dec, 77	0	0	

Total number of students enrolled in
English 102 as of Spring 1981 700

Total number of students enrolled in
102 who failed initial attempt to pass
requirement and course 110

process, its arrangement and appearance complement the workbook developed at Parkside for library use, *Basic Library Skills*. One significant difference from the Dudley model is the nature of the exercises in *Basic College Research*; while each student completes a detailed search strategy based on an individually selected topic, the exercises in each workbook are all the same. By nature of their searches, the students' answers are individual. While most textbooks are dependably similar in the areas concerning research writing (note taking, outlines, quotations, bibliography, etc.), the distinguishing features of *Basic College Research* that set it apart from other texts in the field are the following:

> The statement of university-wide standards as the introduction and guide to completion of the work;
> The use of learning objectives for each chapter;

The use of the instructional mode throughout, directly addressing the student;

The inclusion of a complete, detailed chapter on research strategy — a feature most English or writing texts neglect;

The inclusion of material on evaluation of sources — again a
complete chapter;

The use of specific instruction concerning the process of formulating and writing a thesis that focuses information into a cohesive, persuasive argument successfully reflecting a position
or a point of view relative to an issue, a problem, a topic,
etc.;

The use of checklists that help students spot areas of weakness
and help teachers maintain consistent grading policies
throughout (Figure 4);

The use of a text which balances discussion, examples, and instruction.

One problem faced when developing a series of exercises for a research writing course is that of expenditure of time: students working well should average fifty hours in the preparation of a one-credit
hour course. What kinds of exercises will help them learn, yet not demand time on extraneous work? Each institution, each department,
will select different approaches to answer that question; but a useful rule is this one:

Let the draft of the student's paper evolve from the exercises.

To demonstrate this principle, here is an example from *Basic
College Research*, the chapter "Focus of Argument":

Summarize briefly at least two strong supportive arguments reflecting the position you have taken relative to your topic.
Be sure to indicate the source . . . .

Summarize briefly at least two arguments you may acknowledge
as counterargument. They should reflect a point of view different from the one you adopt toward your thesis.[12]

Basic Library Skills and *Basic College Research* dovetail whether
used in or out of a formal course setting. The final chapter of *BLS*
essentially asks the question: "What are you going to write about
now that you know your way around the library?" After introducing
concepts concerning research in general, and the Collegiate Skills
requirements, *BCR* asks that question again, in the chapter which
introduces search strategy. This is one of the key points in the course
for the librarian and the English faculty member to develop a team

teaching, or at least a guest lecture approach to the content.

For all the machinations of describing a program, a requirement, an approach, such description does not capture the essence of the impetus for this work, nonetheless. The rewards of working together in the classroom have encouraged me to continue working with Patricia Berge; the rewards of helping students learn have given both of us incentive when pressures may have tempted us to stop short of preparing our work for the use of others. *Basic College Research* is growing in popularity among students and faculty; instructors in other departments, particularly women's studies and history, have expressed interest in using it in introductory level courses. Also, the Collegiate Skills Committee now officially recommends its use to students considering the completion of the research writing requirement without taking English 102.

A Look Ahead

Rather than conclude, I would like now to turn to the near future. If the librarian becomes an instructor, he or she must first consider the nature of teaching. If the composition instructor joins forces with the librarian, the tendency may be for both to settle easily and neatly into a methodology which even further separates instruction from teaching. Instruction is based upon the premise that answers must be provided when the appropriate question is asked. It is a form of teaching and indeed, in many cases, may be synonymous with the philosophy or at least the methodology of most teachers. Instructors inform their students: do not spend more than fifteen minutes on this question; if you do, seek help in finding the answer. You have said this, and so have I. But a teacher, from my point of view, is someone who throws a green apple and a red apple into a classroom saying: my premise is that the green apple is sweeter than the red. It is your job to discover the evidence, devise a method for testing my hypothesis, come up with a counter-thesis, provide counter-evidence, and then come back and talk with me. It may take you seconds; then again, it may take your lifetime, and you may die without revealing the crux of your theory, as did Einstein. As Robert H. Bentley of the National Council of Teachers of English points out, the crisis of literacy will lead to a new model, but not to a panacea. Becoming a skilled writer, or researcher for that matter, requires hard work from both teachers and students, and it is a slow, often tedious but certainly incremental process.[13] English teachers, he goes on to say, as custodians of literacy, have a great deal to learn from diverse authorities such as reading specialists, and I might add, from librarians.[14] But we might all do well to learn from those who have considered the nature of learning earlier in time — for, believe it or not, libraries have drawn the needy and the wise on campus for a long time:

> A college library becomes the workshops of the institution, the rendezvous of all the studious, the hearthstone, the heart, and the brain of the whole family. Many a man looks back to it as the place where he learned to think.[15]

Despite the gender-specific reference, this statement by Frederick Vinton, Librarian of the College of New Jersey in 1877, should serve as a well-deserved reminder: the classroom, the objectives, the exercises, should facilitate but not replace learning, and they must not in the process, squelch the enthusiasm flamed by the odd wrong turn on the second floor in the stacks which leads to discovery.

With that *caveat* in mind, what does the future look like? Unquestionably, we have learned much from the efficiency and planning exhibited by faculty and staff in the public schools; similarly, the public schools will inevitably receive benefit from standards set at the college and university level in basic or "collegiate" skills programs. English in the 80s will continue to stress acuity in verbal skills; and as the impact of requirements for research and technical writing skills filters downward through the schools, the English faculty and the librarians will join in stressing mastery of skills related to research gathering and report writing.

Perhaps too, as the concept of team teaching, originating in the public schools, has impacted college teaching in communication fields in the 70s, that impact will also circle back to the junior and senior high school levels so that librarians will, as they increasingly do at the college level, be called upon to augment the faculty member's advising, evaluation, and teaching. Increasingly, the classroom is the library itself.

The link between thought and word, word and work, is to be paramount in the 80s if the past five years are indicators at all; career counselors and personnel directors stress more and more, the need for verbal skills ability. Nevertheless, there are certain warning signals of problems worth sharing with teachers at all levels. Comments fly such as these from students: "But how many periodicals do I have to have in the bibliography?" "All I want to do is pass this requirement, I don't want to learn a new subject." And from faculty: "This course should not have to be taught at all; it should be taught more often, but not by me!"

If creativity is not anathema, literature may be, and that phenomenon is clearly a warning. How will we relate functional skills preparation with changing cultural and sociological directives? How will we relate language and literature at all? We are in some danger of the pitfalls of dualistic thinking if we divorce skills from creative application of those skills; so too, are we in danger of overspecialization of the teacher's role in terms of the practical and technical uses of skills. Also, we are in danger of losing sight of the speculative, humanistic nature of the elements of English — that oddly used term for a nexus of thoughts, experiences, and expressions.

In response to these challenges we may discover anew what English has always been able to do. The linguistic and literary heritage of a culture are interdependent and equally vital. Nevertheless, reality tells us that we cannot always stress them equally in the classroom. But if we bolster the technical and applied end of the spectrum while yielding up the reflective, perceptive end, should we not be challenged? Can we give up hard-won ground for English as the subject which tests experiential knowledge and human values? No; yet we cannot easily relinquish the ground won for the premise that survival depends much upon verbal acuity. We should work very hard not only to train but to nurture students. If we guide students into task mastery, into job security and career paths, we must not fall victim to modish thinking, as I define it: the *gestalt* which perpetuates the belief that new ideas will go away.

New ideas do not go away; they continue to haunt as the powerful images of a multi-cultural society — the language forms and literatures of those cultures. And literature has always been a way of validating not only the experiential but also the theoretical, though we may tend to lose sight of the facts as we worry about how much work to require, what kind of readings to assign, what papers necessary, and how many bibliographic entries there ought to be!

As instructors we exchange the open-ended question for the quantifiable answer, and if we do so, we will eventually have a price to pay in reactionary terms. If we have returned to the basics in the 70s we must return to them again for the challenge and the stimulation of the disturbing question. Literature is and always has been provocative; it provokes us through language. Are we able to accept the Gordion Knot rather than break it, and resist the pressure to isolate, as we "prioritize" in the awful jargon of the past decade? Surely the 80s will call for some integration of the technical and the speculative functions of language. If not, we will face students' increasing verbal skills anxiety as acute as any math anxiety, caused by a restriction of verbal codes to a one-to-one correspondence between intentional meaning and potential significance. We will find an unwillingness on the part of students to express themselves in any but the safest terms, the surest statements about their existence. I have worked with students already demonstrating such "clutching." Self-paced manuals can be written to direct students through the ins and outs of technical mastery, and in fact, they should be available for basic concepts and methods of information gathering and reporting. But such preparation is just that — preparation for future treatment of problems, issues, and for discussion as well. Addressing the eternal verities may be a cliche in the humanities but it is clearly a need in the acronymic world of business and applied technology.

It has gone out of fashion to assign a research paper which discusses a literary work in the composition class, or the research writing class, and alas, even in the literature class! The aim of English teachers has been to provide students with relevant materials for study without burdening them with the terminology of the literary critic. No doubt, similar decisions must be made when assigning the first long papers for students in high school. Yet the English class has always served as major source of verification for personal and experiential knowledge. Hence, we might look again for methods to address writing and research skills towards so-called "literary" issues, better called human issues: not with the intention of giving up or replacing the technical knowledge of writing gained by the methodology of the 70s; but rather, with the intention of applying that expertise towards the formation and sharing of ideas, and experiences.

NOTES

1. University of Wisconsin Basic Skills Subcommittee of Academic Policies Committee, "Basic Skills Program," (Draft) August, 1976, p. 1.

2. Basic Skills Subcommittee Report, Sept. 20, 1978, p. 2.

3. The disadvantage of the "minicourse" is that it does not allow students sufficient time to discover and retrieve materials if interlibrary loan is necessary, or to seek the librarians' advice along the way, as well as the faculty member's. For a model of the minicourse see Marilyn Samuels, "A Mini Course in the Research Paper," *College English* 38:2 (October 1976) 189--93.

4. See Ellen Keever and James Raymond, "Integrated Library Instruction on the University Campus: Experiment at the University of Alabama," *Journal of Academic Librarianship* 2:4 (September 1976), 185--87.

5. For a discussion of Parkside's work in this area, see Carla J. Stoffle, "The Subject Workbook Approach to Teaching Discipline Related Library Research Skills," *Library User: Are New Approaches Needed?* Ed. by Peter K. Fox (London: British Library Research and Development Dept., 1980), pp. 55--64.

BLRD Report No. 5503. London: British Library, 1980.

6. N.A. "A Directory of Library Instruction Programs in Indiana Academic Libraries." ERIC ED 191 487.

7. However, in conversation Ms. Dudley recently (spring, 1981) revealed that some English faculty are offering their services regularly to faculty and classes in other departments as consultants for research writing, and they are serving as readers for student papers in others.

8. However, the efforts by the University of Richmond to develop "research partners" for curriculum development has had a major spin-off program — a self instructional unit for freshman composition classes. Here too, though, the focus is bibliographic instruction. See Dennis Robison and Ernest Bolt, "Five Year Report and Evaluation of the Library Faculty Partnership 1973–1978," University of Virginia at Richmond. ERIC Report ED 181 865.

9. Joyce Merriam, "Helping Students Make the Transition from High School to Academic Library: A Report on a Study of Selected Library Instruction Programs in Mass." ERIC ED 1976 783, pp. 11–12.

10. Carol Lee Saffioti and Patricia Berge, *Basic College Research* (Kenosha: University of Wisconsin-Parkside,1980). The data in Table 1 show a consistent discrepancy between the numbers of students completing the library skills requirement and those completing the research paper requirement, due to several factors including the PSI format for the library skills component of the requirement. Figures were not available at the time of writing concerning the cumulative numbers of students who have failed to write an acceptable research paper unless they attempted the requirement by taking the course. The number of students failing the course does not necessarily reveal the number of students failing the requirement altogether since they have the option of re-submitting a paper independently, or retaking the course. A phone survey conducted last year (1980) polling students who failed English 102 indicated that most students still planned to complete the requirement by retaking the course. Plans are to repeat the phone survey in the summer of 1981 in order to poll students' response to the requirement, the course, and to their competency status.

11. Carol Lee Safioti and Carla J. Stoffle, "Collegiate Rescarch Skills: A Proficiency Based Program," *Wisconsin English Journal* 22:2 (January 1980), pp. 16–22, ERIC ED 153 251.

12. *Basic College Research*, pp. 78, 81.

13. Robert H. Bentley, *WEJ* 22:3 (April, 1978), p. 9.

14. Bentley, pp. 14–15.

15. "Hints for Improved Library Economy, Drawn from Usages at Princeton," *Library Journal* 2:1 (October 1977), p. 53.

THE POLITICS OF ESTABLISHING A MEDIA SKILLS PROGRAM

Thomas Sharrard – Director
Library/Media Services
Wayne-Westland Community Schools

In order to put any educational plan or political strategy into perspective, we must take into consideration substantive social and economic factors that will influence the outcome of our efforts. As those of us working in the field of library media and specifically in K--12 education plan for the future, there are several critical issues that are impacting our ability to make effective decisions. Probably one of the most severe problems affecting our library media programs is the dramatic decline in state and federal support to education. Our school district alone has seen a reduction in our state aid of nearly 50 percent over the last two years. When you take inflation and COLA formulas into account, the loss is even more drastic. Michigan's recession economy and the new attitude in Washington regarding reductions in federal programs do not leave us much room for optimism.

The second major problem that is affecting our school library programs is declining student enrollment. When I started in the Wayne-Westland Schools nine years ago, there were over 24,000 students in our K--12 programs. Our enrollment now stands at a little more than 17,000 and by 1988, we'll be down to 10,700 students. This type of decline is fairly consistent across the nation, but maybe not quite so dramatic as in our state with the compound problem of fewer babies being born and more families moving out of state.

In addition to severe reductions in aid and declining enrollment, we also are involved in a *global* information management crisis. This information crisis may be our salvation in terms of trying to develop programs. Mankind has generated more information in the last year than was generated in the entire history of mankind. We no longer can talk about only books. We are going to have to get involved in the new technologies. The things I have mentioned so far are things that have happened in the last year over which we have no control. We have no control over the fact that there is a significant decline in our students. We have no control over inflation that is eating our budgets and cutting away our staff. There are, however, several things that we can do. We are going to offer you some specific suggestions in terms of survival skills that we have tried.

First of all, let's look at *professional involvement/professional association involvement.* It was almost blasphemy a few years ago to talk about unions. A lot of us are still very uptight about it and universities have been moving very slowly toward professional unionism.

In the past our good planning, well thought out budgets, and formal requests have caused our programs to grow. It's getting down now to the point where this is not enough to establish or even maintain a program. That is specifically what has happened to us in Wayne-Westland Schools. Once a national leader in development of library/media, we have seen a 50 percent reduction in the library program staff. We are now trying to problem solve on how we are going to go ahead and try to implement a library skills program that we developed last year, with half as many people as we had before. That's one of the realities that has happened to us and that's one of the realities that I see that is going to happen in colleges and universities as the pressure comes down and enrollments decline. One of the things you may have thought seriously about is professional association involvement for yourselves and for the people who work for you. One of the real ways we've perceived in trying to save jobs is through specific union contract language. To give you an example, we also have counselors that work in our school system. This year we reduced the counseling staff by one half of a person and we reduced the media staff by nine full time professionals. That tells you what a union contract can do. They have language in their contract that says there will be "x" number of counselors for every so many students in that school. This is one of the realities that you need to deal with in terms of trying to implement a program.

Another real problem that we have been facing is with *role definitions for librarians.* Very frequently, students will come up to the library in the school district and say, "Oh, do you have to have a degree to do that? I didn't know that." There may even be college students that also say that to you. They say this because they see you doing things like picking up paper off the floor, filing catalog cards, checking out books and, it doesn't take a college degree to do that sort of thing. This has to do with this whole area of role definition. If your boss sees you involved mainly in those types of activities he/she may also question the professional salary they are having to pay you!

Curriculum involvement is another critical issue and is one of the things that we have been trying to develop in our school district. We are trying to bring "library skills" into the arena of regular curriculum as one of the "basic skills." It is one of the basic things that we feel that students need to learn. Many of you people in the Michigan area saw the recent issue of the *Detroit News* that talked about the national reading scores and how national reading scores related to inferential thinking had dropped. The example they used was that students were not able to read a catalog card. They talked about the importance of library skills as one of the items they test for inferential thinking. We are trying to implement a program that we tie in with standardized tests. This link becomes even more important as we begin to develop exit testing for high school seniors. The California Achievement Test has been adopted by our school district and we also use the Michigan Educational Assessment Profile. In the last few years, one of the things we've been trying to do is get more "library" items on these tests. There are now a number of items that reflect library skills on these standardized tests and that gives our program a little bit of clout again. If you have union language, you have a little clout. If you have standardized tests, and one of the items that is being measured is your student's ability to read a card catalog or use the *Readers' Guide to Periodical Literature*, then you have a little clout. You can go to the principal, or the administrator, or the dean and say, "Listen, you know we place a lot of importance on these test scores and if we want to improve test scores, we've got to start teaching library skills."

Telecommunications and computer literacy, I think, are also critical to our survival because of growth in technology and the importance of computers. We *are* the computer folks. I mean we're the oldest computer folks. Back in Arabia, thousands of years ago, they started the first library and they first started sorting information into categories so they could access that information. That is a very basic type of computer. We are the information people who have been around for years and therefore, the kinds of technology involved in computers is very integral to what we do. It's really the key that we plug ourselves into technology, in terms of trying to save our library/media programs and trying to make them a more important part of the curriculum. We're trying to key into the fact that we are the information place. We are the information source. The use of computers both by us and by people who come into the libraries is going to be an important service in the next few years. It is no longer enough for a student to be literate. It is *not* enough to know how to read and write. If you know how to read and write, you will not have the skills to achieve any kind of significant success in what some sociologists are calling the Information Society. These scientists have said that this age will have the same importance in terms of impact, that the industrial revolution had on the world. It's no longer enough to know how to read and write. You now have to know how to use a computer terminal whether you are a garage mechanic who has to use computer access for your inventory records or a secretary who needs it as a word processor.

Long-range planning is another important area we very frequently overlook. There is an old saying that when you're up to your tail in alligators, it's hard to remember that your original plan was to drain the swamp. We get too involved in crisis management in terms of our library/media centers, in terms of general operation. That's one of the problems we had in Wayne-Westland, in terms of implementing a library skills program. All the librarians in the buildings were so busy with trying to manage the centers, check out books and doing these other things, we never really got to thinking about the big long-range issues such as whether there should be a sequence of developmental skills as the student enters kindergarten and goes through the elementary to junior to senior high schools. There has to be a transition of developmental, sequential, increasingly complex skills regarding information management processing skills with those students. We've never really dealt with that. We never really dealt with the long term plan. We have now embarked on a joint project with Eastern Michigan University where we're talking about a continuous program from kindergarten right through college to adult learning.

Marketing and public relations is an old theme and another area of concern. You've heard this, I'm sure, at a number of conferences. "If you don't toot your own horn, who will?" You know you're doing a great job down there in the library and once in awhile you peek your head out the door. However, when staff cutting time comes, those library staff who have not had a high visibility PR profile would much more likely be eliminated. Marketing and public relations is again a problem we have faced in Wayne-Westland. As enrollment declines reach the universities, you're going to see the same thing happening in universities that is happening now in high schools. The teachers are literally going out and marketing their classes to encourage students to sign up for them, so they can survive. You're seeing this at Michigan State University. You're seeing this in many high schools already. Literally, what's going to happen is, as the number of students shrink, the same teachers are going to be competing for those fewer students and we librarians are going to be right in there competing with them.

Professional development and role re-definition is a very important concept here too, because the whole thrust of our program in library skills is the theme, "The Librarian as Teacher." This professional librarian is a teacher who is teaching skills; not a clerk, not a janitor, not a pass checker. It is a professional person that has specific knowledge to teach those skills to the students. We're trying to get the librarians involved in more of a teaching role. When we had the original number of librarians that we had before the cuts, we were hoping to increase the amount of instruction in the libraries. Our problem now is having to reshuffle and re-evaluate our situation. With fewer personnel, we're going to have to rely more heavily on the teachers. But we'd still like to have the librarians teaching as much as possible. People should view us as professionals, doing professional duties. That is a very important part of implementing programming and having it stay for a long time.

As I mentioned a few minutes ago, the continuing decline in enrollment is going to significantly affect the colleges in the next five to ten years. We are already having to re-define the kinds of services we offer and the clients that we are trying to service. Basically, what's happening in our particular school district, is, we've had a tremendous emphasis on Adult & Community Education. I think the role of the libraries is changing from a narrow type of approach for the K--12 students to a wider approach. That's why we've changed the theme of our programs from K--12 Library Skills to Preschool through Adult Library Skills. Our program moves from the story-hours and walking the little preschooler to the libraries and getting them acquainted with the fact that they have libraries, straight through our Adult Education Program. This year, we have 12,600 adults and citizens enrolled in our Adult & Community Education Program. Keep in mind that's in relation to 17,000 K--12 students. In the next few years, the two groups are going to equalize.

The same thing is going to happen in the colleges and universities. There no longer will be incoming freshmen just automatically filling the classrooms each year. You are going to have to be out there recruiting and trying to get different services. There is a need for diversification of services that you need to get into whether it be a job training skill, more computer assisted individualized learning, or whatever. What you really need to think about in terms of long-range planning is what you are going to do to keep your program alive and any new services that you want to get involved in that may insure your department's stability. As I mentioned, we have investigated a project with Eastern Michigan University to market a grant proposal to develop some library skills materials that will go all the way from our preschool program right through our adult students. One hundred students a year from our school district attend Eastern Michigan. We feel it would be a very productive venture to tie our programs together to build a life-long sequence of basic library/information processing skills.

The key thing we are emphasizing is that they are *basic skills*. These are survival skills. The process, the handling, the retrieval, the access of information is a survival skill; especially in light of the fact that the amount of information that we have to deal with in the world has doubled in the last year, and may double in the next year. Using our new technology, being able to access information, and having those information processing skills is really what our library program is all about. A lot of the politics of what we've been dealing with is convincing people of that argument, that premise. That is the bottom line basis for implementing this program. But the big issues that are affecting us are the financial issues, the cutbacks, and the fact we're all going to be competing for the same dollar in the next few years. In terms of survival, these are things we have to keep in mind. We must convince people that our programs are an important, critical, integral part of basic education.

OBSERVATIONS FROM A JUNIOR HIGH SCHOOL
MEDIA SPECIALIST

Ed Marman
Marshall Junior High School

Early on, when we decided to plan a coherent sequential library instruction program, we knew that it had to be course-related and subject-related. Because Marshall Junior High School is a feeder school for John Glenn High School, we also wanted a program that would plug in to the excellent library skills program they had developed.

At our junior high school, little politicking was required to institute the program. We first discussed it with the principal who was fairly neutral on the subject. The administration's concept of a librarian was one of a person who acquires, organizes, and distributes library materials. The principal in fact felt that the best person to teach subject research was the teacher. Nonetheless, we obtained administrative cooperation and the program was begun.

In the first stages of discussing what we wanted to do with library instruction on a district-wide basis, we talked of the possibility of eventually requiring mandatory library skills written into the curriculum as an accountable factor. When we discussed this idea with both our science and social science departments at Marshall, they reacted very negatively, feeling that we would, in effect, be telling them what to teach. However, a couple of teachers were intrigued by the idea of having the librarian come into the classroom to teach research skills. One of them asked rather incredulously, "You mean that you would do something for us?" The first feelers of communication were thus established.

Something happened concurrently, quite apart from the formal and sequential library instruction planning activity, which resulted in a totally unanticipated benefit. For the last three years we have been putting approximately 80 percent of our library book funds and any other money we could hustle here and there into the reference collection. While we were developing quite an excellent collection, we felt that the staff were not aware of it or how to use it. We instigated a bibliographic instruction workshop for the teachers.

Because of the size of the staff, we limited the first session to the social studies, English, and science departments. The administration cooperated fully, to the extent of making the workshop mandatory for those teachers. Each teacher was provided with a bibliography of all of the major reference works in the collection, and was required to choose among the newest or most significant to discuss very briefly. Following the oral reports, the librarians turned the staff loose to answer a collective total of 500 questions. The questions were designed and limited to the sources already studied, to guarantee that the teachers used the new and pertinent reference material. We allowed an hour for this process. The maximum number of questions answered by one person was 12. It worked beautifully!

One of the junior high school athletic coaches remained after the session to continue to answer questions, because he was having fun. Another teacher flatly refused to take part in the "hunt" portion of the workshop. He also moonlights selling janitorial supplies. While he wouldn't look up any questions, he did spend two hours going through a set of Thomas' *Register*, which a local business had donated, and found the manufacturers of his supplies. So we won! And *he* won without even knowing it. And four teachers approached the library staff after the workshop, and asked if we would be able to come into the classroom and provide a similar learning experience for the students. And that's how library instruction was actually implemented at Marshall Junior High.

Following up on the teachers' enthusiasm, we designed a format for subject-related instruction. We instigated a four-to-six day unit combining classroom instruction and library exercises to be followed immediately by research assigned by the teacher. On the first day, we go over *Readers' Guide* entries and on the second, we go over reading catalog cards including everything on the card so that students know what is useful to them and what is not. We take the students into the library on the third day for exercises involving questions based on *Readers' Guide* and the catalog. We spend the next day or two going over subject headings and appropriate reference books and follow with a final day of exercises. Throughout we stress use of a search strategy using a simple flow chart. At this point the teacher starts them on research. Students are pre- and post-tested and instruction follows a research guide designed for the subject. We have now done this for environmental science, mammals, Michigan history, and anthropology. Although we have followed the same basic format, changes have obviously been necessary as we find that various approaches work better with some kids than with others. Results of testing showed a fairly consistent increase of about 18 percentage points in students' knowledge of the finding tools and library organization. Just by observing the kids at work, we noticed that they were looking a little harder before asking questions and that their questions were a little more specific. They also seemed to regard the librarians more as teachers. The teachers, all of whom took part in instruction and virtually formed a team with the librarian, felt that while the papers were not written much better, the kids had a little easier time finding information and that the research was more thorough.

Much work remains to be done on format, on beefing up the research guides, and especially on doing more with subject headings. But this will come, we hope. For now, we feel that we have a good start and are greatly encouraged by the willingness of the staff to have library instruction included in their program.

AN OPINION FROM THE FIELD

Rayda Warren
John Glenn High School

A few years ago, even in our high school, I had teachers ask me, "Do you have to have a library degree to do your job?" They were even more surprised when they found out I was also a certified teacher! But in our school, that was in the past, and our teachers now are very educated. Librarians and media specialists know the good things that come forth from that.

As we know, the library setting in the public school is necessarily different than the public library and the university library. Public schools are the first place where formal library instruction for students should take place. We are referring here to "instruction" rather than "orientation." We have found that the orientation approach tends to confuse more than instruct students. We found with high school students that orientations were confusing because they didn't allow for follow-through with skills.

We discovered that library instruction had to be part of the curriculum, and that it had to be made available to all students who wanted it, and even some who didn't. We decided that there was a need for formal library skills sessions integrating library skills into the classroom. Our first step was to approach our building principal and tell him, "This is what's happening! How can we change this? Will you support us?" We found that when approaching an administrator, we were lucky to find one who valued the library instruction program or valued our expertise. Many administrators prefer the media specialists to keep things in order, order the books, and maintain a place to send the kids if they don't have a teacher. So, the first big step, politically, was to obtain support from our administration.

At first, our principal didn't really understand the actual necessity for formal library instruction. But, needless to say, we persevered and we obtained the support. The next step in our process was to go to the building Curriculum Council, the Cabinet, and the department heads. We went to these meetings and explained to them what we felt should happen. We told them that everyone who came into the school in the tenth grade should have instruction. Well, we know that was like asking for the Taj Mahal, but shoot big and you might get something! That was our whole theory in everything we did. We made it so big they were absolutely flabbergasted and we were quite happy with what we ended up with. At first, some of the department heads thought our plan had merit, but nothing really moved.

Our next step was to go to some of the English teachers and help them a little bit in the library with some of their students. We kept pushing and pushing and pushing. "Let me come into your classroom when you're working on something." "Let's make up some lesson plans where we have truly integrated library skills." They really were intimidated because they felt competition. They felt like *we* might be taking over *their* job. As Tom mentioned, this attitude reflects the current situation: it's getting to the point where people are worried about their jobs. To guarantee them, they want to keep control in their area.

We began our integrated library skills process with a debate class. These were all sharp kids. The first decision was how long should we take? I said, "Well, let's take a week." The teacher's response was, "A week! You've got to be kidding!" We got three days. Well, we did a week and then we did two weeks, and then we did three. The teacher was absolutely thrilled because this teacher did not know library skills. We found that some teachers do not have library skills, which says something for the lack of library skills education. The teacher in this case was delighted because we required the teachers to be in every class. Our program does not free a teacher. He/she is required to be there at all times to participate in the entire process. This teacher was thrilled because he learned the library skills and in three weeks, the kids were just absolutely into this. They were learning library skills in direct relation to specific subject area learning. This is why teachers came around to support us: their students were, by using the media center, mastering their subject area content and the teachers were happy.

The teachers did not feel like they were giving up precious time from teaching their subjects, so I think we finally won them over by going into their classrooms. Promise them anything but get into the classes! When the kids finally came into the library, it was just gangbusters. We never had to help them. They knew exactly where everything was. How to use it. What for! Everything! We had a wonderful rapport with these students, because you get to know them and they get to know you and you feel like you're really worthwhile because you're giving those kids instruction: good, useful, hands-on follow-through instruction.

After we initiated our library skills program, we decided to initiate library science classes. We offered three sections, one section per media specialist each semester. This class was for credit and the students had to have a B average or better to enroll. We have relaxed that rule slightly, however, because a lot of "C" students go on to college and make really fine students. Our main concern was that we did not want to get a reputation that the library science course was a "Mickey Mouse" one. That reputation did not happen and so we do get some rather good students.

After a time, word of mouth about good work reached the teachers from department to department. The teachers no longer felt threatened. The teachers had been very uncomfortable being in the classes because of their own lack of library skills. That's the real problem and the competition was a real problem. They felt very threatened by us, at first. And they didn't want to give the class time because they felt they were losing time in the subject area. They found that also was not true.

Our program has been operating for over five years. We were the model for our district program. We are accomplishing good things but what we really need is some research, some data, and some support. I think university librarians could assist in these area particularly by stressing library skills for future teachers. How do we educate people that library science, formal library science instruction is really important? Where does it start? And who is going to do it? Everybody in the whole field needs to be out tooting the horn.

Let's get people educated. We have students coming back from the universities to visit us and they say things like, "Thank God I had your class." They're not intimidated in the libraries anymore. They know what they're about. Our library science classes culminate in a full research paper, so they've gone through the whole process that they will need to use at the university. How can the university librarian play a part in this process? How can you support us? How can we get things rolling so we have a cohesive program? It's an interesting question. We're all in the same boat; we're all just working on different levels. I think it's something we need to consider and think about because we need your support too.

GROUP DISCUSSION GUIDELINES

Some suggestions to consider:

In an effort to come to a consensus within your group as to the current situation as you see it, and the ideal situation as you would like it to be, the group may wish to decide:
--- should school libraries be addressing library education, or should school libraries concentrate on making the library/ media center a comfortable, inviting environment?
--- are students ready to learn library skills at the secondary level?
--- are they actually called upon to learn them? Is teaching library skills mainly a waste of time and effort if the faculty does not require them in the units they teach?
--- should school and academic instruction programs be coordinated? How? Why? Should this instruction be standardized? Can it be?
--- what methods might be implemented to encourage more interaction between school and academic librarians?
--- is the library school the place to begin this interaction?
--- who is to teach the use of the library on the secondary school level? On the beginning college level? Teacher or librarian? A joint responsibility? Where should the instruction occur — the classroom or in the library?
--- how should the library skills be taught? As a separate unit, or integrated? What is ideal? What actually occurs in most schools, colleges and university settings? Should, can, and how are we to change this situation? Who develops and integrates a sequence of library skills, if needed?

Using the George, New Jersey and Calgary models in your registration packet, and referring to the ACRL *Guidelines* also in the packet, discuss the feasibility of these charts. Discuss their practical applications given each participant's environment. Are these realistic? Are the Feagley, Illinois, and Ohio Media Skills tests applicable to your situations?

Can your discussion group reach a consensus on what is to be done in each local situation as each Conference participant returns home? In such a consensus impractical?

(Distributed to Conference participants as a guide to informal discussion sessions and as a prompt to assist in making separate presentations into a more coherent whole.)

PROGRESSIVE LIBRARY CONCEPTS AND SKILLS: ELEMENTARY THROUGH SENIOR HIGH SCHOOL

A Tentative Outline*

I. Elementary level

   A. Concepts

      1. Most intellectual questions do have at least an approximate answer, discoverable by research.
      2. There are various kinds of information.
      3. There are numerous media and formats which carry information.
      4. In order to readily locate specific information, it is efficient to use specially designed factual reference tools.
      5. Certain kinds of information are more readily found in one type of factual reference tool than in others.
      6. There are a few basic principles of arrangement of information within factual reference tools: alphabetical, by category, by date, etc.
      7. Media centers/libraries play an important role in daily life for all citizens.
      8. Media centers/libraries collect all types of information and make it available to all citizens.
      9. The catalog provides several means of knowing what a given media center/library contains.
      10. Media specialists/librarians are helpful, interesting, and rewarding people to deal with.

   B. Skills

      1. Ability to list basic features of the most fundamental types of factual reference tools.
      2. Ability to select an appropriate type of tool to answer a given simple informational question.
      3. Ability to use efficiently 5–10 specific factual reference tools (e.g., telephone directory, dictionary, encyclopedia, almanac, who's who, street map).
      4. Ability to locate specific items within a media center/library, using catalog, floor plans, or other means.

II. Middle school/junior high school level

    A. Concepts: reiterate above, plus

        1. There are variant examples of each type of factual reference tool.
        2. In addition to factual reference tools, there are other "finding" reference tools [bibliographies/indexes] which help identify and locate information within certain media and formats.
        3. Certain types of finding reference tools are more efficient than are others to identify and locate specific kinds of information.
        4. There are a few basic principles of arrangement of finding reference tools.
        5. Most intellectual questions are compound or complex and require being broken down into their simple components before they can be answered.
        6. Similar approaches to information can be used both in formal education and in all other situations requiring information throughout life.

    B. Skills: reiterate above, plus

        1. Ability to describe and use efficiently all types of factual and finding reference tools so far considered, stressing general indexes.
        2. Ability to analyze a compound or complex question into its simple components and suggest appropriate reference tools to solve each.
        3. Ability to identify and locate relevant material within the media center/library on both academic and non-academic topics.

III. Senior high school level

    A. Concepts: reiterate above, plus

        1. Add concepts of reviews, subject bibliographies, and search strategy.
        2. Broaden student expectation to include notion of the existence of specialized media and formats for each subject field, along with correspondingly specialized factual and finding reference tools.
        3. It is possible to choose the most appropriate of several similar reference tools to solve a given question.

B. Skills: reiterate above, plus

1. Ability to outline a basic search strategy for an actual term project on both academic and non-academic topics.
2. Ability to select and use efficiently appropriate reference tools in both the school and public library to carry through a search strategy.
3. Ability to identify relevant resources not available in local libraries and attempt to obtain these elsewhere (from local agencies, academic libraries, legislators, etc.)
4. Ability to communicate effectively with a media specialist/librarian in describing a research project and seeking suggestions.

For post-secondary level, see "Toward Guidelines for Bibliographic Instruction in Academic Libraries," *C & RL News* 36:137–139, 169–171 (May 1975).

----

*Basis for talk given at MAME/MLA Conference, Dearborn, October 1, 1977. The skills indicated are meant to be the basis for behavioral objectives appropriate to each subject and grade level.

Prepared at the University of Michigan Library, February 1978.
by Mary George

REPRINTED WITH PERMISSION OF THE AUTHOR

(Distributed at the Eleventh Annual Library Instruction Conference for discussion purposes.)

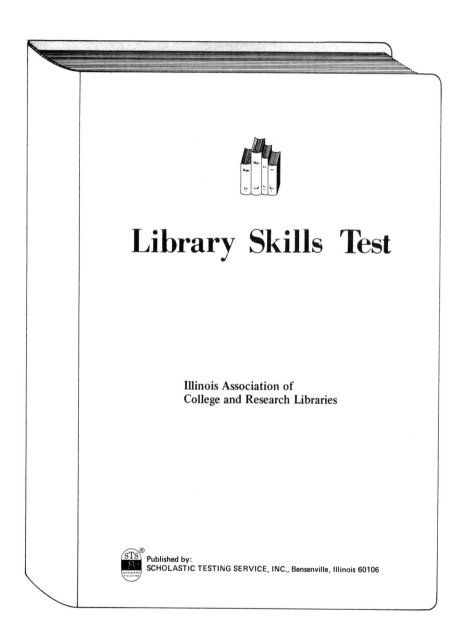

Library Skills Test

Illinois Association of
College and Research Libraries

Published by:
SCHOLASTIC TESTING SERVICE, INC., Bensenville, Illinois 60106

For items 1 to 12 mark on the answer sheet the letter of the response that best matches the definition.

1. A magazine or journal that is issued at regular intervals:
    a) abstract
    b) index
    c) pamphlet
    d) periodical

2. A list of books and other materials which have some relationship to each other:
    a) autobiography
    b) bibliography
    c) biography
    d) footnote

3. An alphabetical listing of topics mentioned in a book, periodical, or other material:
    a) appendix
    b) biography
    c) index
    d) table of contents

4. The history of an individual from birth to death written by another person:
    a) autobiography
    b) bibliography
    c) biography
    d) index

5. A summary of the contents of an article, book, or other material:
    a) abstract
    b) index
    c) pamphlet
    d) periodical

6. Items in great demand (often placed on reading lists) which are available for limited loan periods in a special section of the library or learning resource center:
    a) microform material
    b) newspaper material
    c) reference material
    d) reserve material

7. That place in a library or learning resource center where materials are charged out, returned, etc.:
    a) circulation desk
    b) reference or information desk
    c) periodicals room
    d) stacks area

8. A place in a library or learning resource center staffed by one or more persons whose functions are to answer questions and provide help in using the library:
    a) circulation desk
    b) reference or information desk
    c) periodicals room
    d) stacks area

9. A collection of newspaper clippings, brochures, or other materials of current information on any subject:
    a) audiovisual materials
    b) card catalog
    c) periodical index
    d) vertical or pamphlet file

10. A greatly reduced photographic reproduction of printed matter on film:
    a) audiotape
    b) microform
    c) poster
    d) periodical

11. Non-book items such as sound-recordings, slides, charts, models, etc.:
    a) audiovisual materials
    b) indexes
    c) microforms
    d) reference materials

12. The life of a person written by that person:
    a) autobiography
    b) bibliography
    c) biography
    d) concordance

Go on to the next page.

For items **13** to **19** mark on the answer sheet the letter which identifies the correct term on the catalog card.

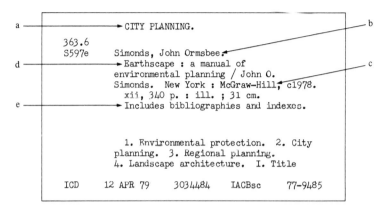

13. The publisher of this book is
    a.   b.   c.   d.   e.

14. The author of this book is
    a.   b.   c.   d.   e.

15. A subject heading for this book is
    a.   b.   c.   d.   e.

16. The title of this book is
    a.   b.   c.   d.   e.

Go on to the next page.

```
┌──────────────────────────────────────────────────────┐
│  301.5                                                 │
│  Ab34h    Abel, Ernest L        , 1943- ◄────────── b │
│              The handwriting on the wall : toward      │
│           a sociology and psychology of graffiti       │
│           / Ernest L. Abel and Barbara E.              │
│           Buckley.  Westport, Conn. : Greenwood        │
│           Press, 1977.◄──────────────────────────── c │
│              156 p. ; 22 cm. (Contributions in         │
│           sociology ; no. 27)                          │
│              Bibliography: p. 147-151.◄──────────── d │
│              Includes index.                           │
│                                                        │
│              1. Graffiti.   2. Popular culture—        │
│           U. S.                    I. Buckley,         │
│           Barbara E         , joint author.            │
│           II. Title     III. Series                    │
│  IU       ac 11-77 MC              UIUUdc    76-50408 ◄── e │
└──────────────────────────────────────────────────────┘
```

a ──►

17. The date of publication of the book is

    a. b. c. d. e.

18. The call number is

    a. b. c. d. e.

```
┌──────────────────────────────────────────────────────┐
│                                                        │
│                                                        │
│     American Indians                                   │
│                                                        │
│         see                                            │
│                                                        │
│             Indians                                    │
│             Indians of North America                   │
│             Indians of South America, etc.             │
│                                                        │
│                                                        │
└──────────────────────────────────────────────────────┘
```

19. The card above means that

    a) all of the terms on the card are subject
       headings used in the card catalog.
    b) "American Indians" is not a subject
       heading in the card catalog but the
       terms below are.
    c) "Indians" is not a subject heading
       used in the card catalog.
    d) these terms are the only subject
       headings used for information related
       to Indians in the Western Hemisphere.

Go on to the next page.

The following lists of call numbers are in the order in which the books would be put on the library shelves. For items 20 to 23, mark on the answer sheet the letter of the response which bests completes each statement.

DEWEY DECIMAL CLASSIFICATION SYSTEM

(a) 959.6	(b) 960.5	(c) 963.73	(d) 965.01	(e) 966	(f) 966.5
B47en	F16c	N523ar	GARD	W244br	St76u

---

20. A book with the call number 966.3 would be placed on the shelf
    Un36f

    a) between (b) and (c).
    b) between (d) and (e).
    c) between (e) and (f).
    d) after (f).

21. A book with the call number 962.78 would be placed on the shelf
    T45ra

    a) between (a) and (b).
    b) between (b) and (c).
    c) between (c) and (d).
    d) after (f).

LIBRARY OF CONGRESS CLASSIFICATION SYSTEM

(a) L	(b) L	(c) LA	(d) LA	(e) LB	(f) LC
112	112	106	205	1028.5	5141
.C62	.N377a	.W7	.B88	.M3	.C76

---

22. A book with the call number L   would be placed on the shelf
                                  1010
                                  .D12

    a) before (a).
    b) between (a) and (b).
    c) between (b) and (c).
    d) between (c) and (d).

23. A book with the call number LA   would be placed on the shelf
                                 8601
                                 .B89

    a) between (b) and (c).
    b) between (c) and (d).
    c) between (d) and (e).
    d) after (f).

Go on to the next page.

For items 24 to 29, mark on the answer sheet the letter of the response which best completes the statement.

24. The part of a book that gives the name of the author, the name of the book, the publisher, and the date and place of publication is the

   a) appendix.
   b) bibliography.
   c) index.
   d) title page.

25. The list of chapters, the subdivisions, and the corresponding page numbers make up the

   a) appendix.
   b) glossary.
   c) index.
   d) table of contents.

26. A list of definitions of difficult or technical words usually found near the end of the book is the

   a) appendix.
   b) bibliography.
   c) glossary.
   d) index.

27. The author or the general editor of a book speaks directly to the readers in the

   a) appendix.
   b) glossary.
   c) preface.
   d) title page.

28. The detailed reference to an original source supporting an important fact or idea in a research paper is the

   a) bibliography.
   b) footnote.
   c) introduction.
   d) preface.

29. In order to determine how thoroughly a topic is covered in a book, look up the topic in the

   a) appendix.
   b) glossary.
   c) index.
   d) preface.

Go on to the next page.

For items **30 to 35**, use this excerpt from *Readers' Guide to Periodical Literature*. **Mark on the answer sheet the responses that best complete the statements.**

SOLAR energy
Scientists urge President: stop reliance on coal and nuclear fuel; Go for development of uniform solar power. J. E. Persico. Sci Digest 82:8-9 + O '77
Sunshine of your life. R. W. Moss. il Sci Digest 82:10-18 + O '77
Toward a solar civilization. F. Von Hippel and R. H. Williams. bibl il Bull Atom Sci 33:12-15 O '77
  See also
Ocean thermal power plants
United States–Energy Research and Development Administration–Ocean Thermal Energy Conversion Program

---

30. How many periodical articles are listed under the subject "solar energy"?

   a) 2
   b) 3
   c) 4
   d) 5

31. Another subject heading in *Readers' Guide* under which you could look to find additional articles on solar energy is

   a) "Ocean thermal power plants."
   b) "Sunshine of your life."
   c) "Coal and nuclear fuel."
   d) "Solar civilization."

The next four questions refer to the circled entry.

32. The title of the periodical in which the circled article appears is

   a) il Bull Atom Sci.
   b) Bull Atom Sci.
   c) il Bull.
   d) F. Von Hippel.

33. The abbreviation "bibl" means

   a) biography.
   b) bibvalent.
   c) biological.
   d) bibliography.

34. The article begins on page

   a) 12.
   b) 33.
   c) 77.
   d) 82.

35. The volume of the periodical is

   a) 12.
   b) 33.
   c) 77.
   d) 82.

For items **36 to 39** use this excerpt from the *New York Times Index*. **Mark on the answer sheet the responses that best complete the statements.**

---

a → **CAPITAL Punishment. See also** Middle East – Israeli-Arab Conflict, Jl 7. Terrorism (General), Jl 7, 14. Personal names NYS Legis to weigh extending death penalty to persons convicted of acts of terrorism (S), Ja 4,44:6
b → Ed on Judge Samuel Conti's comment concerning capital punishment following his sentencing of Sara Jane Moore to life imprisonment for attempted murder of Pres Ford; says Conti's hypothesis that death penalty would deter persons of Moore's bent from resorting to acts of violence cannot be substantiated by history or psychology, Ja 17,24:2

   c   d   c

---

36. The subject heading is

   a.   b.   c.   d.   e.

37. The page on which the article appears is

   a.   b.   c.   d.   e.

38. The column number for the article is

   a.   b.   c.   d.   e.

39. The date of the article is

   a.   b.   c.   d.   e.

Go on to the next page.

172

For items **40** to **43**, mark on the answer sheet the letter of the response which best completes each statement.

40. An almanac is to facts as a thesaurus is to
    a) antonyms.
    b) heteronyms.
    c) homonyms.
    d) synonyms.

41. The reference book which provides the most extensive listing of words in any language is the
    a) abridged dictionary.
    b) biographical dictionary.
    c) geographical dictionary.
    d) unabridged dictionary.

42. Background information needed for a term paper can generally be found in the
    a) dictionary.
    b) encyclopedia.
    c) gazetteer.
    d) handbook.

43. The reference source most likely to provide guidance in locating very current information is the
    a) anthology.
    b) book review index.
    c) encyclopedia.
    d) periodical index.

PART VII
Distinguishing Bibliographic Forms

For items **44** and **45**, use this excerpt from *Biography Index*. **Mark on the answer sheet the letter of the response that best completes the statement.**

> **JOHNSON, Lyndon Baines,** 1908-1973, president
> 1 – Cormier, Frank. LBJ: the way he was. Doubleday '77 276p il pors
> 2 – Drugger, R. LBJ, rampant & couchant. Nation 223:180-2 S 4 '76
> 3 – Graff, H. F. Lyndon B. Johnson: frustrated achiever, (In Power and the presidency. Scribner '76 p 153-63) il pors
> 4 – King, L. L. Machismo in the White House: LBJ and Vietnam. il pors Am Heritage 27:8-13+ Ag '76
> 5 – Lorant, Stefan. Glorious burden. Authors ed. '76 p 811-902. il pors

44. Which of the following entry numbers are for magazine or journal articles about Lyndon Johnson?
    a) 1 and 3
    b) 1, 3, and 4
    c) 2 and 4
    d) 2 and 5

45. Which of the following entry numbers are for books or parts of books about Johnson?
    a) 1 and 3
    b) 1, 3, and 5
    c) 1, 4, and 5
    d) 2 and 4

Library Skills Test

Manual
of
Directions

**Illinois Association of
College and Research Libraries**

Published by:
SCHOLASTIC TESTING SERVICE, INC., Bensenville, Illinois 60106

INTRODUCTION

The *Library Skills Test* is designed to locate students' strengths and weaknesses in working with library materials. The test includes up-to-date items pertaining to current terminology, the card catalog, classification systems, filing, parts of a book, indexes, reference tools, and bibliographic forms used in libraries (or learning resources centers).

The test is designed for use in Grades 7 through 12, and also for use with college freshmen. The goal at each grade level is to locate student misunderstandings which, when corrected, will help the student to work more quickly and more competently with library materials.

The content outline, item numbers, and scoring key are shown on page 4 of this manual. The principal contributors to this test are listed on page 5.

ADMINISTERING THE TEST

The *Library Skills Test* can be given in less than 45 minutes. However, if your school has 40- or 45-minute class periods, students should fill out the information section of their answer sheets on the day *before* the test is given.

Testing Materials

Check your quantities of materials on this chart:

Test booklets – one for each student and teacher...................... _____

STS Analysis of Skills answer sheets – one for each student and teacher .... _____

"Directions" manual – one for each teacher........................... _____

Soft-lead (No. 2) pencils – two for each student. .... _____

The Testing Session

Before class, put on each student's desk – one test booklet
                                       – one answer sheet
                                       – two soft (No. 2) pencils with erasers

After the students are seated, say:

Today we are going to take a test of library skills. The test will show the things you know *well* about using a library, and also the things you do *not* know very well. You will be told about your test results after the tests have been scored.

Pause. Then say:

Please use only a soft-lead No. 2 pencil on your answer sheet. The test-scoring machine can read only those marks made by soft-lead pencils.

Marking the Answer Sheet

Then say:

> Now look at your answer sheet. . . . First, near the top, at the left-hand side, find the word
> "NAME" with an arrow just above it. The arrow points to a row of boxes. . . . We will fill in
> these boxes now. Please print, and print small. First, print your last name, putting one letter
> in each box. . . . Now skip a box, and print your first name — as much as will fit before the
> box marked "MI." Write your middle initial in the "MI" box. Be sure there is a blank box
> between your last name and your first name.

Check that all students have finished before you continue. Then say:

> Now look at the first letter of your last name. In the column below it, find the same letter,
> and fill in the circle for that letter. For example, if your last name begins with an "S," you
> would pencil in the circle with the "S" in it in this first column. . . . Now, go on to pencil in
> the circle for the correct letter in the second column, in the third column, and so on — one for
> each letter of your name. . . . Mark the letters now, but skip the columns that have no letters
> at the top.

Check that all students have finished before you continue. Then say:

> Now, notice the empty circle in each column above the letter A. . . . For each column that has
> no letter at the top, like the blank column between your last name and your first name, pencil
> in the blank circle. Fill in the blank circle in the same way as the other circles, with a heavy
> black mark. . . . Be sure to mark any empty circles between your first name and your middle
> initial.

Check that all students have finished before you continue. Then say:

> Now, double-check your work. Check that you have marked the correct circle for each letter
> of your name. And make sure you have marked the empty circle in each column that has no
> letter at the top.

Pause. Then say:

> As a final double-check, there should be one, and only one, filled-in circle in each column.

Pause. Then say:

> Now, over to the right, at the top, do you see blanks for your school, your grade, and so on?
> We will fill in these blanks now. Please print, and print small. . . . First, print the name of your
> school. . . . Next, print the number of your grade. . . . Next, print your section number if you
> have been given one. . . . Then, in the next row, print the city, state, and zip code of your
> school.

Pause. Then say:

> Then, in the next row, print the word "LIBRARY" in the blank for "SUBJECT TESTED."

Pause. Then say:

> Now, fill in the circle for "BOY" or "GIRL" up at the top — next to the word "SCHOOL."
> Fill in the entire circle with a heavy black mark.

176

Pause. Then say:

> Now, down on the left edge of your answer sheet, find the column of numbers with 7 at the top and 18 at the bottom. . . . Fill in the circle for your grade in school.

Pause. Then say:

> Now you are ready to take the library test.

Marking the Test

Say:

> Find the words "BEGIN TEST HERE" on your answer sheet. They are next to the letter "P" in the name section. . . . Your answer to question 1 will go in space 1 under the words "BEGIN TEST HERE."
>
> There is only one right answer for each question. If you do not know the answer, mark the answer you think is probably right. There is no penalty for guessing.
>
> If you want to change an answer, erase your first answer, and then mark the answer you want. Make all of your marks heavy and black.
>
> All right, open your test booklet and begin. Your answer to question 1 goes in space 1 under the words "BEGIN TEST HERE." Go right on to the end of the test.

Allow the students a maximum of 30 minutes to complete the test. When the time is up, or when all students have finished, call time.

Collect the test booklets in one pile, and the answer sheets in a separate pile.

RETURNING THE TEST MATERIALS

Make a separate pile of answer sheets *by grade* for the students in your school — a pile for Grade 7, a pile for Grade 8, etc.

Next, put a paper band (not paper clips or rubber bands) around each pile of answer sheets.

Then, ship the answer sheets in the cartons provided. The answer sheets should be shipped by priority mail to:

> SCHOLASTIC TESTING SERVICE, INC.
> 62 Weldon Parkway
> Maryland Heights, Missouri 63043

Finally, return the test booklets, by fourth-class mail, to:

> SCHOLASTIC TESTING SERVICE, INC.
> 480 Meyer Road
> Bensenville, Illinois 60106

Item No.	Skill Area	Scoring Key	Item No.	Skill Area	Scoring Key
PART I.	**USING LIBRARY TERMINOLOGY:**		**PART IV.**	**RECOGNIZING THE PARTS OF A BOOK:**	
1.	"Periodical"	D	24.	Title page	D
2.	"Bibliography"	B	25.	Table of contents	D
3.	"Index"	C	26.	Glossary	C
4.	"Biography"	C	27.	Preface	C
5.	"Abstract"	A	28.	Footnote	B
6.	"Reserve Material"	D	29.	Index	C
7.	"Circulation Desk"	A			
8.	"Reference or Information Desk"	B	**PART V.**	**INTERPRETING AN INDEX:**	
9.	"Vertical or Pamphlet File"	D	30.	Number of references	B
10.	"Microform"	B	31.	Cross references	A
11.	"Audiovisual Materials"	A	32.	Title of a periodical	B
12.	"Autobiography"	A	33.	Abbreviations	D
			34.	Page numbers	A
			35.	Volume of a periodical	B
PART II.	**INTERPRETING CATALOG CARDS:**		36.	N.Y. Times Index: Subject headings	A
13.	Publisher of the book	C	37.	N.Y. Times Index: Page numbers	D
14.	Author of the book	B	38.	N.Y. Times Index: Column numbers	E
15.	Subject of the book	A	39.	N.Y. Times Index: Dates	C
16.	Title of the book	D			
17.	Publication date of the book	C	**PART VI.**	**USING REFERENCE SOURCES:**	
18.	Call number of the book	A	40.	A thesaurus	D
19.	Headings on cards	B	41.	An unabridged dictionary	D
			42.	An encyclopedia	B
PART III.	**ARRANGING CALL NUMBERS:**		43.	A periodical index	D
20.	Dewey Decimal System	C			
21.	Dewey Decimal System	B	**PART VII.**	**DISTINGUISHING BIBLIOGRAPHIC FORMS:**	
22.	Library of Congress System	C	44.	Magazine (journal) articles	C
23.	Library of Congress System	C	45.	Books; parts of books	B

178

PRINCIPAL CONTRIBUTORS TO THE LIBRARY SKILLS TEST

Susan Brandehoff
Formerly Assistant to the Director of
Technical Services
University of Illinois
Urbana, Illinois

Melissa Cain
Assistant Professor of Library Administration
University of Illinois
Urbana, Illinois

Eileen Dubin
Associate Head of Circulation
Northern Illinois University
DeKalb, Illinois

Elaine Hart
Instruction Librarian
DePaul University
Chicago, Illinois

Judy Harwood
Undergraduate Librarian
Southern Illinois University
Carbondale, Illinois

Larry A. Miller
Assistant Librarian for Public Services
Moraine Valley Community College
Palos Hills, Illinois

OTHER CONTRIBUTORS TO THE LIBRARY SKILLS TEST

Carol Barry, Elmhurst College, Elmhurst, Illinois
Joyce Bennett, Sangamon State University, Springfield, Illinois
Richard Higginbotham, Northeastern Illinois University, Chicago
Jeri Oltman, Carl Sandburg College, Orland Park, Illinois
Roland Person, Southern Illinois University, Carbondale, Illinois

Library Skills Test

COLLEGE NORMS – ILLINOIS COLLEGE STUDENTS

Scholastic Testing Service, in cooperation with the Illinois Library Association, has developed norms for 1200 college students in the state of Illinois. This population of 1200 students represented the following colleges:

Private Colleges:

Aurora College	50
Elmhurst College	100

Community Colleges:

Carl Sandburg College	100
Kishwaukee College	100
Lincoln Land Community College	100
Moraine Valley Community College	100
Oakton College	50

State Universities:

Illinois State University	100
Northeastern Illinois University	150
Northern Illinois University	200
Western Illinois University	150

Total	1200

The study focused on the skills of college freshmen, although a few sophomores were included in several of the test populations. The students in each college represented a sample from that college, either (a) because the entire freshman class was tested from which a random sample of answer sheets was drawn, or (b) because a sample of freshman English classes was tested from which a random sample of answer sheets was drawn.

Instructional Needs Analysis

An Instructional Needs Analysis – "rights analysis" – is shown on pages 2 and 3 of this report. This analysis shows the percent of the 1200 students marking each item correctly. Highlights of the analysis show that these students were most skilled on items 8, 13, 14, 27, and 36, while they experienced the greatest difficulty on items 5, 22, 37, 44, and 45.

The Instructional Needs Analysis is set up in worksheet form to help other schools compare their "rights analysis" data with those of the Illinois group.

Published by
Scholastic Testing Service, Inc., 480 Meyer Road, Bensenville Illinois 60106

Student Norms

In this Illinois study student raw scores ranged from a low of 7 to a high of 45. Ten of the 1200 students attained a perfect raw score of 45. The median (middle) score was 35 items correct.

Norms for the Illinois students are shown on page 4 of this report. The norms table shows percentile-rank scores and stanine scores for the distribution of raw scores.

Descriptive Statistics

The mean in this Illinois study was 34.6, with a standard deviation of 6.1. Alpha (reliability) coefficients for the eleven colleges ranged from .630 to .883, with a median of .777. The alpha coefficient for the eleven colleges combined was .833, which yielded a standard error of measurement of 2.48 raw-score points (N = 1200).

INSTRUCTIONAL NEEDS ANALYSIS

PERCENT-CORRECT BY ITEM

			ILLINOIS STUDENTS	LOCAL GROUP	LOCAL GROUP
PART I. LIBRARY TERMINOLOGY					
1.	"Periodical"	D	90%		
2.	"Bibliography"	B	79%		
3.	"Index"	C	64%		
4.	"Biography"	C	73%		
5.	"Abstract"	A	50%		
6.	"Reserve Material"	D	73%		
7.	"Circulation Desk"	A	91%		
8.	"Reference or Information Desk"	B	96%		
9.	"Vertical or Pamphlet File"	D	75%		
10.	"Microform"	B	90%		
11.	"Audiovisual Materials"	A	94%		
12.	"Autobiography"	A	85%		
PART II. CATALOG CARDS					
13.	Publisher of the book	C	98%		
14.	Author of the book	B	98%		
15.	Subject of the book	A	65%		
16.	Title of the book	D	65%		
17.	Publication date of the book	C	85%		
18.	Call number of the book	A	89%		
19.	Headings on cards	B	63%		
PART III. CALL NUMBERS					
20.	Dewey Decimal System	C	86%		
21.	Dewey Decimal System	B	89%		
22.	Library of Congress System	C	35%		
23.	Library of Congress System	C	80%		

2

Score Interpretations

The authors suggest the following interpretations which can later be modified in light of local experiences:

College students scoring in the 40-45 range can be expected to work effectively with routine vocabulary and interpretation of basic tools. Even these students, however, will probably benefit from some brief instruction on strategy or process of using information sources for major research projects.

College students scoring in the 33-39 range will probably need special help when working on other than routine projects.

College students scoring below 33 cannot be expected to function efficiently in the library. Group instruction, perhaps using this test as a curriculum guide, is clearly needed for such students.

INSTRUCTIONAL NEEDS ANALYSIS — continued

PERCENT-CORRECT BY ITEM

		ILLINOIS STUDENTS	LOCAL GROUP	LOCAL GROUP
PART IV. PARTS OF A BOOK				
24. Title page	D	76%		
25. Table of contents	D	88%		
26. Glossary	C	88%		
27. Preface	C	95%		
28. Footnote	B	85%		
29. Index	C	56%		
PART V. INDEXES				
30. Number of references	B	66%		
31. Cross references	A	82%		
32. Title of a periodical	B	75%		
33. Abbreviations	D	89%		
34. Page numbers	A	92%		
35. Volume of a periodical	B	86%		
36. N.Y. Times: Subject headings	A	97%		
37. N.Y. Times: Page numbers	D	51%		
38. N.Y. Times: Column numbers	E	54%		
39. N.Y. Times: Dates	C	85%		
PART VI. REFERENCE SOURCES				
40. A thesaurus	D	58%		
41. An unabridged dictionary	D	64%		
42. An encyclopedia	B	87%		
43. A periodical index	D	84%		
PART VII. BIBLIOGRAPHIC FORMS				
44. Magazine (journal) articles	C	46%		
45. Books; parts of books	B	47%		

3

STUDENT NORMS

– ILLINOIS COLLEGE STUDENTS –

Raw Score	Percentile Rank	Stanine
45	99	9
44	99	9
43	98	9
42	94	8
41	90	8
40	84	7
39	78	7
38	71	6
37	64	6
36	57	5
35	49	5
34	43	5
33	38	4
32	31	4
31	26	4
30	22	3
29	18	3
28	15	3
27	12	3
26	9	2
25	8	2
24	7	2
23	6	2
22	5	2
21	4	1
20	3	1
19	2	1
18	2	1
17	1	1
16	1	1
1-15	1	1

Mean = 34.6	Median Score = 35
SD = 6.1	Chance Score = 11

Alpha Coefficient = .833
SE meas = 2.48

(N = 1200)

4

LIBRARY SKILLS QUIZ
Bucknell University
Bertrand Library

NOTE: This final questionnaire departs from the rest of the orientation testing program in that the results of this questionnaire will not be confidential. The Library staff is interested in assisting those students who may need help with library skills. Therefore, your results will be transmitted to the Library staff who then will be in a better position to help you.

PLEASE PRINT ONE ANSWER TO EACH QUESTION ON THE ACCOMPANYING ANSWER SHEET.

A. Directions: This is a reproduction of an actual card from the card catalog. Refer to it when answering the following questions:

```
                The poverty of power

HD9502
.A2C643   Commoner, Barry, 1917-
 1976        The poverty of power : energy and the
          economic crisis / Barry Commoner. 1st
          ed. New York : Knopf : distributed by
          Random House, 1976.
             314 p. ; 22 cm.
             Includes bibliographical references
          and index.


             1. Power resources.  2. Power
          (Mechanics)  3. Energy policy--United
          States.  4. United States--Economic
          policy--1971-      5. Economic history.
          I. Title

PLeb                           PLUbut      75-J6788
```

1. In what year was this book published?

2. What is the entire call number of this book?

Administered to new students during Orientation each Fall

Reprinted with permission of the author

3. Would this particular card be found in the card catalog under "H," "P," "C," or "T"?

4. Can cards for this book be found in the catalog under the following? (Answer YES or NO)

    a. Commoner, Barry   [the author of the book]
    b. Energy and the economic crisis   [the subtitle]
    c. Energy Policy – United States   [the subject]
    d. Knopf   [the publisher]

B. Directions: Use this excerpt from the *Readers' Guide to Periodical Literature* to answer the questions below.

1. What is the proper subject heading to look under for articles on solar eclipses?

2. To find related articles on solar energy, what other subject heading is suggested?

3. Which article under Solar Energy Industry is illustrated?

    a. "Squeeze on funds for solar energy."
    b. "Solar from Germany."

4. What is the number of the volume of *Forbes Magazine* containing the article "Harnessing the Sun"?

5. On what page does this article begin?

C. Matching Exercise.   Directions: Enter on the answer sheet the letter of the library source (right column) most closely corresponding to each numbered definition (left column).
Note: there is one extra entry in the right column!

1. a magazine

2. a guide to periodical articles with summaries of the articles.

3. photographic reproduction in reduced size

4. a guide to periodical articles without summaries of the articles

5. a reference book with synonyms

6. a list of books

a. Art Index

b. Art Journal

c. Roget's Thesaurus

d. Microfiche

e. Bibliography of American Literature

f. Psychological Abstracts

g. Current Biography

LIBRARY SKILLS QUIZ

Answer Sheet

Name _____   Student No. ____
       (Print last name, first name)

A. Card Catalog

1. _____ 2. [ ]   3. Circle one: H P C T

4. Circle one: Yes   Yes   Yes   Yes
          a)   b)   c)   d)
             No   No   No   No

B. *Readers' Guide to Periodical Literature*

1. _____   2. _____

3. Circle one: a b   4. _____   5. _____

C. Matching Exercise

1. ___   2. ___   3. ___   4. ___   5. ___   6. ___

LIBRARY SKILLS PRE-TEST
ANNE ROBERTS, SUNY ALBANY

I. Arrange the following call numbers in the order you would expect to find the books so labeled on the library shelves.

A. HF	B. DA	C. Z
5838	4679	21
D5	A9	B44
1975	1958	1967
D. DA	E. HF	F. HQ
4697	5383	1426
A76	D23	B69
	1972	

1. _____

2. _____

3. _____

4. _____

5. _____

6. _____

II. Arrange the following titles in the order in which you would expect them to appear in the card catalogue.

A. *The Old Man and the Sea*   1. _____

B. *To the Lighthouse*   2. _____

C. *Operating Manual for Spaceship Earth*   3. _____

D. *On the Experience of Time*   4. _____

E. *Tortilla Flat*   5. _____

III. According to the following excerpts from *Library of Congress Subject Headings*, could you expect to find the subject heading "Photographic Wastes" in the card catalogue? _____

Reprinted with permission of the author

Photographic surveying *(TA593)*
  sa Aerial photogrammetry
    Photographic interpretation
  x Phototopography
  xx Photogrammetric pictures
    Photogrammetry
    Photography—Scientific applications
    Surveying
  Note under Photogrammetry
  — Mathematical models *(TA593)*
  — Tables
Photographic wastes
  See Photography—Wastes, Recovery of
Photographing of court proceedings
  See Conduct of court proceedings
Photographs
  sa Aerial photographs

IV. Using the numbers that label the diagram below, identify the following parts of the catalog card:

A. call number _____   B. author _____
C. title _____   D. publication date _____

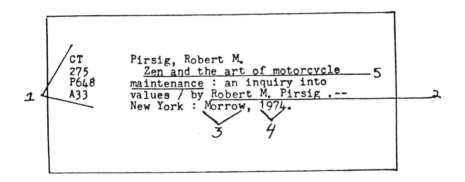

V. Using the numbers that label the diagram below, identify the following elements of the periodical index entry:

A. title of article _____   D. periodical title _____
B. author _____   E. volume number _____
C. subject _____   F. date of issue _____

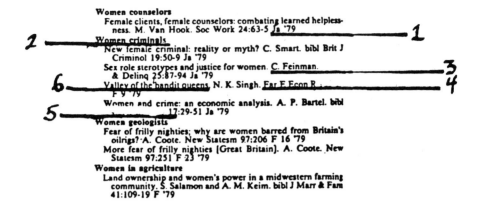

Women counselors
Female clients, female counselors: combating learned helplessness. M. Van Hook. Soc Work 24:63-5 Ja '79

Women criminals
New female criminal: reality or myth? C. Smart. bibl Brit J Criminol 19:50-9 Ja '79
Sex role sterotypes and justice for women. C. Feinman. & Delinq 25:87-94 Ja '79
Valley of the bandit queens, N. K. Singh. Far E Econ R F 9 '79
Women and crime: an economic analysis. A. P. Bartel. bibl 17:29-51 Ja '79

Women geologists
Fear of frilly nighties; why are women barred from Britain's oilrigs? A. Coote. New Statesm 97:206 F 16 '79
More fear of frilly nighties [Great Britain]. A. Coote. New Statesm 97:251 F 23 '79

Women in agriculture
Land ownership and women's power in a midwestern farming community. S. Salamon and A. M. Keim. bibl J Marr & Fam 41:109-19 F '79

VI. In the following situations, briefly describe what steps you would take and what sources you would consult in the library to locate the information asked for.

A. Your psychology professor asks you to compile a list of twenty recent journal articles about the use of behavior modification with retarded children.

B. You are interested in learning more about passive solar heat and want to know if the U.S. Government has any reports about its efficiency or plans for building a passive solar house.

C. Allen Ginsberg has been invited to give a poetry reading at the university. As a reporter for the *ASP*, you are assigned to write a biographical sketch of Ginsberg to appear in the newspaper the day before the reading.

D. For a paper about the recent political changes in Nicaragua, you want some information about the civil war that led up to the change in government.

KNOWLEDGE OF THE LIBRARY SEARCH PROCESS

DePauw University
Roy West Library

Developed under the auspices of
the Council on Library Resources

You are provided LIBRARY AREA identification names (right-hand column). Each library identification name is given an IDENTIFICATION NUMBER (left-hand column).

IDENTIFICATION NUMBER	LIBRARY AREA
1	Card Catalog
2	Index Area
3	Reference Area
4	Rotary File of Periodical Holdings
5	Periodicals Reading Room
6	*New York Times* & Index
7	Government Documents
8	Abstracts

DIRECTIONS:

In the following exercise, read each item carefully. Decide which area of the library (LIBRARY AREA) is the most logical place to *start* your search for the information described in the item. Respond to each item by placing the IDENTIFICATION NUMBER of your choice in the blank preceding it.

EXAMPLE:

__1__ Moss, Pete, *Better Gardens*

After reading this item your decision is that the card catalog is the area in which to start your library search. The identification number for the card catalog is "1": therefore, you place a "1" in the blank preceding "Moss, Pete . . . . "

Reprinted with permission of the author

ITEMS:

_____ 1. Wilson, John Arthur, *Modern Practice in Leather Manufacturing*

_____ 2. Census data on Putnam County, Indiana.

_____ 3. A current *Newsweek* for browsing.

_____ 4. Summaries of doctoral dissertations

_____ 5. You want to make a current comparison of the *Indianapolis Star* and the *Chicago Tribune*

_____ 6. *Games People Play*

_____ 7. Congressional debates on thc Alaskan pipelines

_____ 8. Who's who in the humanities

_____ 9. A professor sends you to read an article in May 1975 *Society*

_____ 10. Watchmaking information to check out of the library

_____ 11. Look again at an article you read several months ago on wildcat oil drilling

_____ 12. *Dictionary of Angels*

_____ 13. Does the library subscribe to *Ms., Ebony,* or *Time?*

_____ 14. Book with a Superintendent of Documents classification number

_____ 15. Find current information on the fad of tie-dyeing

_____ 16. Supreme Court decision on abortion

_____ 17. Birthdates for Albert Schweitzer and Lawrence Welk

_____ 18. Day-by-day coverage of the Kent State 'incident'

_____ 19. Magazine article on ESP

_____ 20. Review in a magazine on Alistair Cooke's book, *America*

_____ 21. Bibliography of resources on Black Americans

_____ 22. Ten longest bridges in the world

_____ 23. Organization chart of the U.S. Postal Service

_____ 24. List of colleges offering degrees in Chicano Studies

****

Developed in 1976--1977 under a Library Service Enhancement Program grant.

COLLEGE ENTRANCE LIBRARY ORIENTATION TEST

Donnelley Library
Lake Forest College

Here is a college entrance level quiz which will help you to discover what you know about a college library. The results will make librarians aware of the ways in which students can be helped in using the library.

Your Name _____ Advisor's Name _____

I. YOUR BACKGROUND:

1. What kind of library have you used most during the last two years? (Check appropriate line)

    ____ a. High School   ____c. College or   ____d. Other
                                    university   (specify)
    ____ b. Public   ____e. None

2. What kind of call number did that library use for its books?

    ____ a. Dewey   ____b. Library of   ____c. Other (can you
                              Congress   specify?)
          Example: Example:
          327.77   LB   ____d. Don't know
          K72C   2386
                            .B69

3. Name a book you've read recently_____

II. CARD CATALOG

A. Call numbers (1)

Lake Forest College Libraries use the Library of Congress classification system. It is arranged alphabetically on the first line, numerically on the second, and in order by letters and decimal numbers on the third. Here are several sets of numbers. Put a check in the blank before the set which is in the correct order.

Reprinted with permission of the author

	a.	DA	DA	D	D	D
____		17	23	62	62	12
		.E45	.E6	.S2	.S16	.M78

	b.	D	D	DA	DA	DC
____		126	62	1795	1795	12
		.S19	.S2	.E6	.E45	.M78

	c.	D	D	DA	DA	DC
____		62	126	1795	1795	12
		.S2	.S19	.E45	.E6	.M78

B. The best way to find out if the library has a copy of:

___ (2) Fitch, John. *An Introduction to Educational Administration.* New York: Random House, 1972.

___ (3) Fitch, John. "Testing in the Schools," *Learning Today* 45: 331--332.

___ (4) Fitch, John. "Test Administration in Schools" in Smith, John, ed., *Tests and Measurements.* New York: Macmillan, 1973.

Is to look in:
(Put letter in blank)

a. Author-Title catalog under Fitch

b. Author-Title catalog under Smith

c. Subject catalog under Smith

d. Subject catalog under Education

e. List of journals in the College Library under *Learning Today*

f. List of journals in the College Library under Fitch

g. Don't know

C. CATALOG CARD: To make sure you understand the essential information on a catalog card, examine this one and then fill in the blanks below. [Card example on next page.]

Mr. ____ ____ ____(5), who was born in the year ___ (6) has written a book entitled ____ ____ ____ (7). It was published in the city of __ ____ (8) by ___ ,____ , and ____ (9) in the year ___ (10). It has __ (11) pages of introduction and ___(12) pages of text. There is a ____ (13) on pages 227--234. The call number is ___/__/__(14). Subject cards for this book are found under the headings ____ ____(15) and ____(16). There is also a card in the catalog under the____(17).

D. SUBJECT CARD CATALOG: You are looking for a book on the Civil War. What would be the best topic to look under in the subject card catalog? Make a check in the appropriate blank. (18)

____ (A) War Between the States
____ (B) United States — History — Civil War
____ (C) Civil War
____ (D) Wars — America — Civil — 1865

III. USE OF PERIODICAL INDEXES

A. You may know the *Readers' Guide to Periodical Literature* already. It is important because it indexes widely read periodicals and because it is a model for many other more specialized indexes. To test your comprehension of the *Readers' Guide*, read this and fill in the blanks below.

AUTOMATIC turntables. See Phonograph—Record changers

AUTOMOBILE drivers
   Auto breaks! Isometric and stretching exercises. H. D. Loucks and D. L. Loucks. il Fam Health 8:47-8 My '76
   50 street survival tips. J. McGraw. il Hot Rod 29:85-7+ Je '76

   See also
Chauffeurs

The second article about automobile drivers entitled _____
_____(19) is written by__ _____ (20). It appears in volume
___(21) of _____ (22) on pages ___-___ (23) in the issue
dated ___ , _____(24).
For other closely related articles, consult the subject heading __(25).
If you wanted to find information about automatic turntables, what
subject heading would you look under in this index? _____ (26).

  B. To find the complete periodical title, look in:
      (Check the appropriate blank) (27)

      _____   a. The front of the periodical index
      _____   b. A dictionary
      _____   c. The card catalog

IV. IDENTIFY LIBRARY TERMS AND SOURCES

Match these terms with the definitions on the right by placing
the appropriate letter in the blank. Some answers may be used
more than once.

___ *Who's Who*	(28)	a.	Biographies
___ Atlas	(29)	b.	A list of books, journal
___ *Readers' Guide*	(30)		articles, or other materials
___ Thesaurus	(31)	c.	Periodical index
___ Abstract	(32)	d.	A topic to look under in
___ Bibliography	(33)		the card catalog or index
___ Subject heading	(34)	e.	Synonyms
___ Periodical	(35)	f.	Magazine
___ *Biography Index*	(36)	g.	Summary
___ *Encyclopedia of*	(37)	h.	Geographical locations
Associations		i.	Reviews of recent non-
___ *American Art*	(38)		fiction
Directory		j.	List of organizations
___ Annual	(39)	k.	Addresses of schools of
___ *Current Book Re-*	(40)		design
view Citations		l.	A type of publication
___ Journal	(41)		issued once a year

V. SEARCH STRATEGY

You have been assigned to do a research paper on a topic that's
new to you. Write the number of the set of approaches that
would be the best _____(42).

1. Find an encyclopedia article
   Use a text book bibliography
   Use a periodical index
2. Use a subject bibliography
   Consult a librarian
   Look at the current periodicals shelf
3. Browse in the stacks in your general subject
   Ask a friend who took the course before
   Check the card catalog

******

HOW THIS TEST IS USED:

Lake Forest College has administered a Library Skills quiz to entering freshmen for the last six years. This test is given during the pre-school orientation period, in conjunction with a writing skills test in which students provide a sample of their writing for analysis. While these writing samples are being examined by a brace of English instructors, the library test is corrected immediately by the library staff, and the results of both tests are coded and sent to advisors. If students score poorly in library skills, we suggest that faculty recommend the English Composition course, available to about two-thirds of the registered freshmen. Each course section contains a component which introduces the students to library research using a set of guides which has been prepared by the librarians.

Our skills test is based on the Feagley-Columbia University test, though one of its many variations. During its use, the text has been changed slightly as we have become aware of deficiencies or ambiguities in it. We have recently adopted a format which we feel gives the appearance of a standardized test, and therefore it is regarded more seriously by students.

Although the test's primary purpose is to determine which students should be advised to take the composition course, it is used for several other reasons. It alerts the community (students and faculty alike) to the importance of library use. It makes the freshman aware that he does have some things to learn about using the library, as few students achieve perfect scores.

It has been our intention at Lake Forest College to make use of the test to help us evaluate our instruction. As yet, the test has not proved to be the kind of measurement instrument which could be used as a pre- and post-test for English Composition or other beginning courses. However, as part of our instructional program in the Humanities, we are analyzing our questions to develop a more effective measurement of student learning in courses which have integrated library research.

LIBRARY ORIENTATION
AND
INSTRUCTION — 1980

Hannelore B. Rader
Director, Library/Learning Center,
University of Wisconsin--Parkside

The following annotated bibliography of materials on orienting users to the library and on instructing them in the use of reference and other resources covers publications from 1980. Several items from 1979 were included because information about them had not been available in time for the 1980 listing. Some entries were not annotated because the compiler was unable to secure a copy of the item.

The bibliography includes publications on user instruction in all types of libraries and for all types of users from young children to adults. To facilitate the use of the list, it has been divided into categories by type of library.

Even though the library literature includes many citations to items on user instruction in foreign countries, this bibliography includes only publications in the English language.

Interest in library use instruction continues to be strong even though the number of publications is down 36% from 1979. All categories show a decrease as compared to last year:

academic libraries	23%
public libraries	80%
school libraries	43%
special libraries	71%
all levels	20%

Again it can be noted that some of the items appear in non-library publications. Growing concern with user instruction for data base searching is evident in the increasing number of items on this topic. Even though there are still many publications on program descriptions, a growing number of the listed citations are of a theoretical nature and concern themselves with integrating library use instruction into the curricula of schools and academic institutions as well as the future of library use instruction in view of budget cuts and retrenchments.

COMMUNITY COLLEGE LIBRARIES

Bender, David R. *Learning Resources and the Instructional Program in Community Colleges.* Hamden, CT: Library Professional Publishers: Shoe String Press, 1980.

Cammack, Floyd and others. *Community Library Instruction. Training for Self-Reliance in Basic Library Use.* Hamden, CT; Linnet Books, 1979.

This book describes the library instruction program at Leeward Community College in Hawaii. It gives the history and development of the program including the formulating of objectives, development of materials and testing mechanisms. Also included are a variety of appendices such as memos to faculty. A lengthy bibliography covering 1965–1978 on library instruction in colleges and universities is also given.

Cupp, Christian M. *Library Handbook.* ERIC Document Reproduction Service, 1979. ED 176 814.

This is a handbook for students, staff and community users of the Southeastern Community College Library in North Carolina to help them gain skills in using the library. Orientation as well as library instruction information is included.

Voit, Betty and Joan Tribble. "The Workbook Approach to Teaching Basic Library Skills in the Community College: Two Points of View." *Kentucky Library Association Bulletin* 44 (Winter, 1980), pp. 4–8.

Describes the use of an adapted version of M. Dudley's and C. Stoffle's workbooks which is used with English composition classes at Jefferson Community College. Since the fall of 1979 all students in this course are required to complete the workbook. Also included is an opinion of one of the English instructors.

COLLEGE AND UNIVERSITY LIBRARIES

Adams, Mignon. "Individualized Approach to Learning Library Skills." *Library Trends* 29 (Summer, 1980): 83--94.

Explains the concept of individualized instruction approach to library use instruction. Discusses the use of signs, guides, tutorials, programmed instruction, computer-assisted instruction and others.

Andrews, Phyllis. "A University Approach to Bibliographic Instruction." *Bookmark* 38 (Fall, 1979): 219–224.

Describes the development and growth of the University of Rochester Library instruction program since 1976. Discusses factors such as needs assessment, staff training, student participation and the future.

Bailey, Lucille E. "Bibliographic Instruction at Hunter College: Past, Present and Future." *Bookmark* 38 (Fall, 1979): 257–260.

Describes the history of library instruction at Hunter College where a separate department of library instruction was created in 1970. Outreach to freshmen in English courses, both regular and skill-oriented, is emphasized at Hunter College. Course-related instruction to upper class members and graduate students is also part of the library instruction program.

Beaubien, Anne K. *Bibliographic Instruction within Library and Discipline Associations: A Survey of Contact Persons and Committees.* ERIC Document Reproduction Service, 1979. ED 175 468.

This survey, conducted under the auspices of the Bibliographic Instruction Section of the American Library Association — Association for College and Research Libraries, identifies groups within the library and other professional associations concerned with bibliographic instruction. Addresses and contact persons for identified bibliographic instruction interest groups are included.

Bhullar, Pushpajit and Harold V. Hosel. *Library Skills.* ERIC Document Reproduction Service, 1979. ED 190 083.

This is a workbook used in a basic library skills course at the University of Missouri and other research courses. It provides basic instruction in library use and research. Each chapter includes individual assignments.

Bibliographic Instruction Handbook. ERIC Document Reproduction Service, 1979. ED 188 623.

This handbook published by the American Library Association, Association of College and Research Libraries Bibliographic Instruction Section is based on the ACRL *Guidelines for Bibliographic Instruction.* It was reported on in last year's Library Orientation and Instruction Bibliography in *Reference Services Review.*

Biggs, Mary. "A Proposal for Course-Related Library Instruction."

School Library Journal (January, 1980): 34–37.

Author lists essentials for effective course-related library instruction based on her library instruction experiences at the University of Evansville at Indiana. Also discusses which type of library skills should be taught to beginning undergraduates and/ or high school students.

Blythe, Hal and Charlie Sweet. "Vampire in the Stacks: A Video Production that Demystifies the Library." *Media and Methods* 17 (December, 1980): 29–30.

At Eastern Kentucky University students are introduced to the library, its services and some research skills through a videotape called "Dick and Jane Visit the Library" using the vampire theme.

Byrne, Frederick. "Undergraduate Library Instruction at Columbia." *Bookmark* 38 (Fall, 1979): 253–256.

Discusses course-related library instruction to undergraduates at Columbia University. Library exercises are used with freshmen English students. The program reaches almost all of these students. Course-related instruction is also provided to upperclass students. Individual consultations with a librarian are also available. Teaching aids have been developed.

Cipolla, Katherine. "M.I.T.'s Point-of-Use Concept: A Five-Year Update." *Journal of Academic Librarianship* 5 (January,1980): 326–328.

The author describes the point-of-use library instruction program developed at MIT from 1969–1973 which was called Project Intrex and supported by a grant from the Council on Library Resources. Since that time the program has changed somewhat in scope and format. To keep such a program effective target audience, topic, financial and technical resources and educational purpose must be taken into consideration. Particular attention must be paid to workable equipment, revisions and upkeep of the program.

D'Aniello, Charles A. *Monograph Bibliography Building in History.* ERIC Document Reproduction Service, 1980.

Presents history reference works for research purposes. Includes sections on guides to and sources for bibliographies, information on how to evaluate and use bibliographies and sources. Also recommends research handbooks and information on using Interlibrary Loan and the Center for Research Libraries.

Darrell, Bob. "A Faculty Survey of Undergraduate Reading and Writing Needs." *Peabody Journal of Education* 57 (January, 1980): 85–93.

Dudley, Miriam. "Teachers and Librarians: Partners in Library Instruction." *Catholic Library World* 52 (July–August, 1980): 17–21.
>   Author describes library instruction in school systems and the lack of librarian-teacher partnerships. Various methods of instructing students in library use are briefly outlined and the workbook method used at UCLA is discussed in detail.

Elkins, Elizabeth and Jacqueline Morris. "Bibliographic Instruction in New York Academic Libraries." *Bookmark* 38 (Fall, 1979): 211–218.
>   Discusses some terms and methods of library instruction as well as reasons for renewed interest in this area of librarianship. Gives function and objectives of the New York Library Instruction Clearinghouse and discusses the data collected in the 1976 Directory on library instruction in academic libraries compiled by that clearinghouse.

First Annual Progress Report on the Course-Related Library Instruction Program. ERIC Document Reproduction Service, 1979. ED 184 581.
>   This is a description of the first year progress on a 3-year National Endowment for the Humanities and Council on Library Resources funded grant program to integrate library instruction into humanities courses. Emphasis was given to English composition courses at Ball State University.

Fox, Peter. *Library User Education; Are New Approaches Needed?* Proceedings of a Conference, Trinity College, Cambridge, 1979. London: British Library, 1980. (Research and Development Report No. 5503.)
>   This volume contains fourteen papers, group discussion summaries and a conference summary by Peter Taylor. Peter Fox discusses "Higher Education in Britain and the U.S.: Implications for User Education." Geoffrey Cubbin talks about "Fresh Priorities in Library User Education" while Colin Harris addresses himself to "User Needs and User Education." Sharon Hogan's paper is on "Educating Librarians for User Education in the U.S., or Who Is Teaching Us to Teach?" Nancy H. Aberle's presentation is on "Information Package on Teaching and Learning Mehods for Librarians." "Cooperation: The Challenge Before Us" is the

topic of Patricia S. Breivik's paper. John Cowley discusses "User Education in the Traditional Library." The British library instruction clearinghouse is discussed by Charles Crossley and Carolyn Kirkendall gives a presentation of the American counterpart. "Of Workbooks and Whirlwinds" is the topic of Mimi Dudley's presentation, followed by Carla Stoffle with "The Subject Workbook Approach to Teaching Discipline-Related Library Research Skills" and Daphne Clark's "Aids for User Education: Packages." Patricia Culkin relates information on "CAI and Instruction in the Use of Computerized Systems" followed by Michael Brittain's "Instruction in the Handling of Information: Some Possible Developments." "Academic Libraries and Undergraduate Education: the CLR Experience" is discussed by Nancy Gwinn and Terry Connor presents "Review of Past Research."

Gruber, James and others. *Materials and Methods for Sociological Research*. New York: Neal-Schuman Publishers, Inc., 1980.

This workbook is intended for undergraduates to teach them methods of information gathering and types of information sources for research and independent study in sociology. Each chapter provides objectives and an exercise.

Gwinn, Nancy. "Academic Libraries and Undergraduate Education: The CLR Experience." *College and Research Libraries* 41 (January, 1980): 5--16.

The article describes Council on Library Resources-funded programs relating to library instruction and encouraging library-faculty cooperation in a 10-year period, 1970–1980. Results and problems with many of these CLR--NEH funded programs are discussed.

Hallman, Clark N. *A Library Instruction Program for Beginning Undergraduates*. ERIC Document Reproduction Service, 1980. ED 188 633.

This describes a program at the University of Nebraska designed by librarians to introduce undergraduates to the use of the library. The program includes AV presentations, a library orientation workbook and exercises and is used by faculty to introduce their students to library skills. All materials are included.

Herstein, Sheila. "Team Teaching and Bibliographic Instruction." *Bookmark* 38 (Fall, 1979): 225--227.

Discusses the positive aspects of cooperative teaching involving both librarian and faculty members in integrated library instruction. Provides some effective teaching methods for bibliographic instruction.

Hogan, Sharon A. "Training and Education of Library Instruction Librarians." *Library Trends* 29 (Summer, 1980): 105--126.

Discusses the training of librarians for providing library use instruction via continuing education, workshops, seminars and some formal education through library schools' offerings.

Hughes, Phyllis and Arthur Flandreau. "Tutorial Library Instruction: The Freshman Program at Berea College." *Journal of Academic Librarianship* 6 (May, 1980): 91–94.

At Berea College freshman-level bibliographic instruction has been provided on a tutorial basis for five years. This program instructs large numbers of freshmen in bibliographic searching skills on a one-to-one basis. The program is described in its entirety.

Johnson, Kathleen A. and Barbara S. Plake. "Evaluation of PLATO Library Instruction Lessons: Another View." *Journal of Academic Librarianship* 6 (July, 1980): 154--158

The authors report on a project to assess the effectiveness of teaching library skills to freshmen via computer-assisted instruction utilizing PLATO tutorials and the traditional tour. The project took place at the University of Nebraska--Lincoln in 1977/78 in cooperation with four English composition instructors. Pre- and post-tests were given. Results indicate that the PLATO and tutorial were somewhat more effective than the traditional tour or no instruction. Cost factors restrict further use of the PLATO system. This study is also compared with a similar study at the University of Illinois at Urbana-Champaign.

Kessler, Ridley R. "Documents Bibliographic Instruction." *North Carolina Librarian* 38 (Fall, 1980): 28–32.

Discusses how to plan a program to teach the use of documents by using goals and needs of students. This should be followed by good publicity. Also given is a list of what to teach in such a program.

Kilpatrick, Janet L. "Quality of Student Research Enriched by Librarian/Faculty Cooperation." *North Carolina Librarian* 38 (Fall, 1980): 9--13.

Library research skills can help prepare students for a lifetime of self-directed learning and problem-solving. Librarians and faculty can cooperate to teach library research skills to students. An example is provided from East Carolina University where physical education students participate in a graduate research course taught jointly by a faculty member and a librarian.

Kirk, Thomas and others. "Structuring Services and Facilities for Library Instruction." *Library Trends* 29 (Summer, 1980): 39--53.

Discusses administrative and pedagogical issues relating to library instruction programs presuming that such a program would be an essential program of an academic library. Utilizes a review of the literature to discuss various library instruction parts relating to services and facilities.

Kirkendall, Carolyn. "Library Instruction. A Column of Opinion." *Journal of Academic Librarianship* 6 (March, 1980): 40--41.

Responses are elicited on the future of library use instruction from Better Paulk, Valdosta State College; Betty Hacker, Colorado State University; R.E. Walther, Ambassador College; Carla Stoffle, University of Wisconsin-Parkside, and Alan Erickson, Harvard University.

Kirkendall, Carolyn. "Library Instruction. A Column of Opinion." *Journal of Academic Librarianship* 6 (May, 1980): 96--97.

Reactions are provided to the problem that all library instruction results from faculty requests. William Prince from SUNY--Buffalo, Wayne Meyer from Ball State University, Maureen Pastine from the University of Illinois, Janice Koyama from California State University, Long Beach and Carol Ahmad from Oklahoma State University responded.

Kirkendall, Carolyn. "Library Instruction. A Column of Opinion." *Journal of Academic Librarianship* 6 (July, 1980): 160--161.

This column solicits reaction to a comment that most library instruction programs are "FLOPS" and that the faculty needs to be educated first. Respondents include Beth Shapiro from Michigan State University, Joan Worley from the University of Tennessee--Knoxville, Ilene Rockman from California Polytechnic State University and Virginia Parr from the University of Oregon.

Kirkendall, Carolyn. "Library Instruction. A Column of Opinion." *Journal of Academic Librarianship* 6 (September, 1980): 220--221.

A variety of answers are given to the question "how can you prevent the instruction librarian from becoming burnt out from repetition and overwork?" Respondents include Penelope Pillsbury from the University of Vermont, Heather Lloyd from Oklahoma State University, Tim Schobert from the University of Ottawa, Anita Evans from Michigan State University, and Karen

S. Seibert from the University of Illinois at Chicago Circle.

Kirkendall, Carolyn. "Library Instruction. A Column of Opinion." *Journal of Academic Librarianship* 6 (November, 1980): 282–283.

Mildred Kirsner from Miami-Dade Community College – North Campus reacts to "why are most instruction librarians young?" David Isaacson from Western Michigan University discusses the need for student research skills. Approaches to instruction are outlined by Thomas W. Atkins from Baruch College. "Does Success Depend on Personality" is answered by Kay Langston from the University of Illinois at Urbana-Champaign and Deborah C. Masters from SUNY-Albany. Joan Chambers from the University of California--San Diego responds to the burnout issue. Floyd Cammack from Leeward Community College discusses how to obtain faculty support.

Kirkendall, Carolyn. "Library Use Education: Current Practices and Trends." *Library Trends* 29 (Summer, 1980): 29–37.

From her vantage point as Director of Project LOEX, the national clearinghouse for library instruction materials, the author discusses the status of library instruction in academic libraries, problems, methods, materials and planning. Included are some thoughts on future trends.

Kirkendall, Carolyn. *Reform and Renewal in Higher Education: Implications for Library Instruction.* Ann Arbor, Michigan: Pierian Press, 1980.

These are the papers from the Ninth Annual Conference on Library Orientation for Academic Libraries held at Eastern Michigan University, May 3–4, 1979. Subjects covered relate to changes in the higher education curriculum. Sheila Hart from Harvard University discusses the core curriculum and the library. Katherine Jordan from Northern Virginia Community College describes how community college librarians can become catalysts for curriculum change. Richard Dougherty from the University of Michigan talks about administrative and budget support for library instruction. Library instruction and communication with the faculty are related in the paper presented by Joann Lee from Lake Forest College. Academic librarians' changing roles and expectations are elaborated upon by A.P. Marshall from Eastern Michigan University. Cleo Treadway and Josephine Bradley from Tusculum College discuss the four R's – implications for library services. Strategies for promoting library instruction are outlined by Charles Brownson from Christopher Newport

College. Ruth Foley from St. Clair County Community College addresses curriculum and the community college library. How to keep pace with change is discussed briefly by Ann Neville from the University of Texas at Austin. The LOEX report is provided by Carolyn Kirkendall and the annual review of the library instruction literature by Hannelore Rader concludes this small volume.

Knapp, Sara. "Instructing Library Patrons about Online Reference Services." *Bookmark* 38 (Fall, 1979): 237--242.

Presents an overview of SUNY--Albany's user education relating to online reference service. It is felt that this type of instruction should be part of the total library instruction. Describes the use of media in instruction about online services and the content of such instruction.

Kochtanek, Thomas R. *Measuring the Effectiveness of a Library Skills Program.* ERIC Document Reproduction Service, 1980. ED 190 157.

This summarizes the impact of a library skills course for undergraduates using pre and post tests on a sample of 55 students. Improvements for the card which covered terminology and catalog, subject headings, reference materials, biography and indexes and for the tests are suggested.

Koren, Stefania A. "Student Library Internship Program: Manhattanville's Approach to Bibliographic Instruction." *Bookmark* 38 (Fall, 1979): 243–248.

Describes Manhattanville College's bibliographic instruction program which is integrated into the curriculum. The curriculum has two interesting features which made the integration of library instruction into it a possibility: the Preceptorial (required reading and writing skills) and the Portfolio (independent work, bibliography, research, critical thinking). Student-Library Interns are utilized in the program. Discusses continuation and evaluation of the program.

Lawrence, Gail H. "The Computer as an Instructional Device: New Directions for Library User Education." *Library Trends* 29 (Summer, 1980): 139--152.

This paper points out the future of information access, shows some practices that detract from this future and takes a look at the implications of automation for library user education.

Lowry, Glenn R. *Online Document Retrieval System Education for*

Undergraduates: Rationale Content and Observations. ERIC Document Reproduction Service, 1980. ED 183 176.

The conceptual content and hands-on activities of a course in online information retrieval skills are described. This course is for undergraduate students at Stockton State College as part of the undergraduate computer science curricula. Included are evaluations and references.

Lynch, Beverly and Karen Seibert. "The Involvement of the Librarian in the Total Educational Process." *Library Trends* 29 (Summer, 1980): 127–138.

Discusses library use by students as influenced by curriculum, educational theory and teaching methods changes from the 1880s to the present. Relates library instruction to the mission and curriculum of various academic institutions and shows the important role college presidents and chancellors can play in the integration of library and curriculum.

McNeil, Don W. *Academic Library Instruction: The Use of Films; the Use of Educational Television; the Use of Audio Learning; the Use of Programmed Learning; the Use of Visual Learning Material. Occasional Papers No. 5–9.* ERIC Document Reproduction Service, 1980. ED 190 135.

This is a collection of five papers which provide librarians with information on using various instructional media formats in library instruction. Included in each paper are overviews, research, related information, a summary and a bibliography.

Melhado, L. Lee. "Chemical Composition." *Journal of Chemical Education.* 57 (February, 1980): 127–128.

At the University of Illinois at Urbana undergraduates in science curricula have the opportunity to take a course called "Technical Writing and the Chemical Literature" which helps them to gain writing and literature searching skills. Included in the course are computer searching techniques. Seventeen writing assignments are given, 15 require library use.

Miller, Carolyn. "The Round-Robin Library Tour." *Journal of Academic Librarianship* 6 (September, 1980): 215–218.

At the Capitol Campus of the Pennsylvania State University librarians have developed the Round-Robin Library Tour which provides both orientation and significant interaction between librarians, staff and users. The plan is built upon moving groups of students to different stations in the library where they receive a 5-minute talk by different librarians.

Morgan, V.E. "Library Instruction for Education Students at Hong Kong University." *Education Libraries Bulletin* 23 (1980): 22--30.

Describes a program of library instruction for education students at the University of Hong Kong during 1978--79. Also gives evaluation of the program's progress by library staff, teaching staff and students.

Morris, Jacqueline M. *Bibliographic Instruction in Academic Libraries. A Review of the Literature and Selected Bibliography.* ERIC Document Reproductive Service, 1979. ED 180 505.

Provided here is an overview of bibliographic instruction in academic libraries, an indexing language for literature searches and a 174-item bibliography.

Natoli, Joseph P. "An Enemy in the Camp: The Academic Librarian and Academic Structure." *North Carolina Libraries* 38 (Fall, 1980): 5--7.

Author discusses faculty's monopoly on providing students with knowledge through lectures, classes, assignments and other academic procedures. This often makes students lose interest in learning. Teaching often takes place in a vacuum. Librarians could become linkers in the learning process.

O'Donnel, Michael. "Library Instruction during a Period of Retrenchment." *Bookmark* 38 (Fall, 1979): 231--236.

Discusses how the merger of Richmond College and Staten Island Community College in 1976 to become the College of Staten Island affected library instruction. Librarians on each campus developed separate philosophies of library instruction in relationship to orientation tours, credit-bearing instruction and bibliographic instruction.

Patterson, Thomas H. "Library Skills Workshops for Support Personnel." *RQ* 19 (Summer, 1980): 351--353.

This article describes a library skills program at the University of Maine at Orono which is specifically directed at faculty secretaries, administrative assistants, clerk-typists and other academic support staff. The program includes orientation to the library, instruction in the use of the card catalog and indexes as well as information on copyright, reference and circulation services, ordering of materials, computer searching and interlibrary loan.

Piele, Linda and others. *Materials and Methods for Business Research*

New York: Neal-Schuman Publishers, Inc., 1980.

The purpose of this workbook is to teach undergraduates methods of information gathering and types of information sources for research and independent study in business. Each chapter is built around objectives and incorporates an assignment.

Reeves, Pamela. *Library Services for Non-Traditional Students. Final Report*. ERIC Document Reproduction Service, 1979. ED 184 550.

The program involved an assessment of library needs, use and services for non-traditional students at Eastern Michigan University and the development of credit library skills course for non-traditional students, e.g., students who had been out of school for several years. Pre and post tests showed that students who took this course improved their library skills substantially, that non-traditional students did not differ significantly from others in success with the course and that taking the library skills course did not significantly affect success in other courses taken concurrently. Survey and test instruments are included.

Roberts, Anne. "The Changing Role of the Academic Instruction Librarian." *Catholic Library World* 51 (February, 1980): 283-285.

Author discusses the new, active role academic librarians can play in the campus environment particularly through involvement in library instruction. Librarians are participating more actively in the educational process, are mediators between students and faculty, can help bring about needed change on campus and can improve communication on campus.

Roberts, Anne. "How to Generate User Interest in Library Orientation and Instruction: Some Practical Suggestions." *Bookmark* 38 (Fall, 1979): 228–230.

Discusses value of user instruction and defines it. Provides information on how to plan and publicize a user instruction program and how important the timing of instruction is. Emphasizes the importance of keeping statistics on instruction activities.

Roberts, Anne. *Organizing and Managing a Library Instruction Program. Checklists*. ERIC Document Reproduction Service, 1979. ED 176 731.

These 12 checklists were published by the American Library Association, Association for College and Research Libraries,

Bibliographic Instruction Section and are intended to help academic librarians in the development of library instruction programs.

Robison, Dennis E. and Ernest C. Bolt, Jr. *Five-Year Report and Evaluation of the Library-Faculty Partnership Project: 1973-- 1978.* ERIC Document Reproduction Service, 1980: ED 181 865.

This report describes a five-year program at the University of Richmond to promote cooperation between the library and academic programs toward increasing student use of the library through faculty development and bibliographic instruction. Faculty members were given release time to develop library-oriented teaching approaches.

Rogers, Sharon. "Research Strategies: Bibliographic Instruction for Undergraduates." *Library Trends* 29 (Summer, 1980): 69–81.

Defines research strategy in terms of undergraduate students' needs for library instruction. Discusses the issue of whether to teach students sources or process.

Senzig, Donna. "Bibliographic Instruction in the Discipline Associations." *College and Research Libraries News* 41 (November, 1980): 297--298.

Discusses a method of involving faculty in library instruction through the professional associations of their subject disciplines. The ACRL Bibliographic Section Cooperation Committee did a survey and discovered that librarians are involved in 30 professional associations in the humanities and social sciences. Ways for librarians to become involved in professional associations are described.

Shilstone, Marian. "Faculty and the Academic Library." *Connecticut Libraries* 21 (Spring, 1979): 39--40.

The author reports the results of a questionnaire which was sent to academic librarians in 18 academic libraries in Connecticut to assess librarian/faculty communication, collection development cooperation, bibliographic instruction cooperation and special problems in library-faculty relations. The communication between librarians and faculty can occur through curriculum committee membership and the faculty library committee was one of the various findings reported.

Smith, B.J. "State of Library User Instruction in Colleges and

Universities in the United States." *Peabody Journal of Education* 58 (October, 1980): 15--21.

The author provides an overview of library user instruction in academic libraries in the U.S. by describing development in this area in the 70s. She focuses on clearinghouses, professional association activities, librarians' training for user education, terminology, teaching methods and problems.

Stewart, Frances. "Teaching Library Usage Through Programmed Instruction at Alabama A & M University." *The Alabama Librarian* 32 (November--December, 1980): 8--11.

A course in library instruction at the Alabama A & M University was designed to aid freshmen in gaining necessary library skills. The course consists of 10 modules on videotape. Students are given behavioral objectives, overall competency, rationale, goals, pre-assessment, activities and post assessment.

Stottle, Carla J. and Judith M. Pryor. "Competency-Based Education and Library Instruction." *Library Trends* 29 (Summer, 1980): 55--67.

Provides a detailed definition of competency-based education and the role of library instruction in it based on the experiences at the University of Wisconsin-Parkside.

Tucker, John M. *Articles on Library Instruction in Colleges and Universities, 1876--1932*. University of Illinois, Graduate School of Library Science. Occasional Papers 143, February, 1980.

This annotated bibliography lists journal articles on library use instruction in academic institutions in the United States from 1876 to 1932. It provides a retrospective viewpoint on the topic of library instruction.

Tucker, John M. "User Education in Academic Libraries: A Century in Retrospect." *Library Trends* 29 (Summer, 1980): 9--27.

Gives an historical overview of library use instruction from 1840 to the present relating it to educational theories of each period and other social influences.

Werking, Richard H. "Evaluating Bibliographic Education: A Review and Critique." *Library Trends* 29 (Summer, 1980): 153--172.

Discusses the need as well as the reason for and methods of evaluation of library use instruction. Presents information on using tests, surveys, illuminative evaluation and statistics to assess the impact of library instruction.

Wood, Richard J. *Vacation College: An Opportunity for Librarians.* ERIC Document Reproduction Service, 1979. ED 181 913.

The vacation college concept is based on leisure and life long learning of recreational activities along with a library skills program. The one-week course is taught in a relaxed manner and provides library information for persons on vacation and out of school through discussions and audio visual materials. The appendix includes a brief questionnaire, a participant's handbook and a bibliography.

PUBLIC LIBRARIES

Tarakan, Sheldon. "Opening the Attic Door: Bibliographic (and other) Instruction at the Port Washington Public Library." *Bookmark* 38 (Fall, 1979): 249–252.

Describes the Port Washington Public Library's program of library orientation and instruction on an individual basis and through mini courses. Training and the use of videotapes and services to the Spanish speaking children, young adults and sophisticated users supplement the program.

SCHOOL LIBRARIES

Bantly, Harold A. and Janet L. Freedman. *Information Searching. A Handbook for Designing and Creating Instructional Programs.* ERIC Document Reproduction Service, 1979. ED 188 632.

This is a guide for librarians and media specialists to design and develop library instruction programs for high school and college students. Included is information on need assessment, program goals and objectives, sample instructional materials and course outlines and evaluation guidelines. Descriptions of instructional methods are given.

Bernstein, Helene C. *A Comparison between the Library Skill Knowledge of Two Eighth Grade Student Groups with the Added Variable of Practical Library Experience.* ERIC Document Reproduction Service, 1980. ED 188 154.

This is a report of a study to determine if the library skills knowledge of students who had practical library experience along with classroom instruction would be significantly greater than that of students who had only classroom instruction and no library experience. The study was done with two groups of eighth grade students. Pre tests were used and both groups received 16 weeks of instrucion in library skills but only one group of students was provided with a 40-minute per week library experience period to apply the newly learned skills. All students were post tested. No significant differences of the two programs were found after the test results were compared. Tests and worksheet are included in appendix.

Brake, Terence. "Educating for Access into the Information Culture." *Education Libraries Bulletin* 23 (1980): 1–14.
    The author maintains that user education in schools must be changed completely if it is to be effective. Teachers must be trained to introduce and reinforce library skills in day-to-day teaching. A project has been undertaken under the auspices of the British Library Research and Development to set up information skills in the Curriculum Research Unit. This unit is placed in its educational context to help design the future of education where students will be educated to gain access to and control of the ever-increasing information explosion.

Brumback, Elsie L. "The School Media Program: The Alpha and Omega of Life-Long Bibliographic Skills." *North Carolina Librarian* 38 (Fall, 1980): 14–27.
    Discusses the Educational Media Competency Goals and Performance Indicators by the North Carolina State Department of Public Instruction to be implemented by all schools in order to teach students life-long bibliographic and media skills.

"Celebrate the Library." *Early Years* 10 (April, 1980): 68–70.
    Discusses the library skills program for grades K–6 in the Grosse Pointe, Michigan school system. The program is based on sequential development and periodic review and in cooperation with the social studies curriculum.

Christine, Emma R. "Curriculum Design Competencies for School Librarians." *International Library Review* 12 (October, 1980): 343–357.
    The school librarian should be trained to become part of the teaching process and the curriculum development process in the school in order to help develop the full potential for learning in all children. Curriculum responsibilities for school librarians are discussed.

Claver, Sister Peter. "Librarians as Motivators." *Catholic Library World* 52 (July–August, 1980): 13–16.
    Author discusses the need to help children develop skills to become independent and critical users of research materials. Librarians and teachers can become motivators to children in the

effort to teach them how to become independent thinkers even in elementary school. The library can be used as a laboratory with hands-on experience and even critical thinking can be taught in the lowest levels.

Coles, M.H. and C. White. "Libraries and Laboratories." *School Science Review* 61 (June, 1980): 682–689.
    Provides information on how to acquire library skills in high school through science courses and gives an example of a science-based library course.

Davies, Ruth A. *The School Library Media Program: Instructional Force for Excellence.* 3d ed. New York: Bowker, 1980.

Dequin, Henry C. and Jane Smith. "Learning Disabled Students Can Be Tutors in Library Media Skills." *Top of the News* 36 (Summer, 1980): 352–356.
    A study was conducted in 1979 at Coventry Elementary School in Illinois to determine to what extent learning disabled elementary school students can be trained in basic library and media skills and to what extent these trained students can tutor younger regular students to perform these skills. It was found that learning disabled elementary school children can be trained to perform basic library skills and can be effective tutors to younger regular students in performing such skills.

Dermott, R. Allan and others. "Searching for Clues among the Stacks: A Motivational Library Skills Program that Works." *Reading Psychology* 1 (Fall, 1979): 41–46.
    Gives a description of a week-long library skills program for disadvantaged high school students using a game approach. The game is described in detail.

Herring, James E. "User Education in Schools." *The School Librarian* 28 (December, 1980): 341–345.
    The purpose of user education is described as a process which enables pupils to locate and use information sources. Problems with user education stem from the low participation of teachers in user education and user education not being a part of the curriculum. Several solutions are offered. Future potentials are pointed out.

Irving, Ann. "Innocents Abroad: Information Concepts and Skills for the International Child." *Education Libraries Bulletin* 23 (1980): 15–21.

Describes a feasibility study for UNESCO through the International Federation of Library Association's Section on School Libraries to develop the concept of information skills in children. International materials related to this concept were identified and suggestions are given to fill identified gaps in these materials.

"Learning Skills: Elementary." *Curriculum Review* 19 (February, 1980): 20--26.

Gives a review of eight instructional kits, supplementary texts and professional references for K--8 library and study skill instruction.

"Learning Skills: Secondary." *Curriculum Review* 19 (Feburary, 1980); 27--37.

Reviews twelve instructional kits, supplementary texts and professional references to teach library and study skills in secondary schools.

Marland, Michael. "Tough on Assignments." *Times Educational Supplement* July 7, 1980, p. 11.

Gives a comparison of school librarians in the United States and in the United Kingdom. The author visited the U.S. to study school library skills instruction. He found a great variance from one school to the next. In some schools library skills are well integrated into the curriculum and taught on a progressive basis. Some teacher appraisals were even found to include specific reference to the class teacher's utilization of library media. But more often he found the school librarian quite isolated from the educational process. He concludes that in both countries there is a problem with assignments made up by teachers which do not utilize library and media skills.

Merriam, Joyce. *Helping Students Make the Transition from High School to Academic Library: A Report on a Study of Selected Library Instruction Programs in Massachusetts*. ERIC Document Reproduction Service, 1979. ED 176 783.

Reports on a study of existing library instruction programs in secondary schools in Massachusetts to assist students to make the transition from high school to academic libraries. Library instruction in high school was compared to that in the University of Massachusetts at Amherst. Recommendations for program changes are given. Appendices include information on schools involved in the study, program descriptions and a chart comparing the resources in school libraries with those in a university library.

Oldfield, Phyllis. "Initial Teacher Training in Library Usage: A Survey." *The School Librarian* 28 (June, 1980): 120-124.

British teachers and teacher training institutions were surveyed to discover how many teachers had received what type of library skills education which would help them to educate pupils in library skills. Results indicate much more needs to be done to train teachers in this area.

Roberts, Jean. "Checking Out Library Resources." *Teacher* 98 (August, 1980): 58-59.

Gives guidelines for teacher-librarian cooperation to plan assignments which require library use and to plan tours of libraries.

Simon, Rose. "Library Use Instruction: Curricular Support or Curricular Integration?" *North Carolina Libraries* 38 (Fall, 1980): 4.

The editor discusses the librarians' relationship to the curriculum and how they are usually supporting it but not very deeply involved in it in spite of their wish to be teachers, too.

Smith, Jane B. *Library Skills for Middle Grades*. ERIC Document Reproduction Service, 1980: ED 186 014.

This is a guide for teachers of library skills to elementary school students. Activities are provided to orient students to the library and to teach them basic library skills.

Vandergrift, Kay E. *The Teaching Role of the School Media Specialist*. Chicago: American Association of School Librarians, ALA, 1979.

This monograph discusses the teaching role of the media specialist, their cooperation with other teaching staff, their role in staff development and their involvement in evaluation of students.

Wagner, Diane S. and J. Rosenfeld. "Teaching in Tandem: Media Specialist/Librarian and the Classroom Teacher." *Reading Horizons* 20 (Winter, 1980): 99-102.

Describes a process to develop a library and media skills program for elementary school students through the cooperation of school librarians and English teachers. The process was tried in a southern New Jersey school system where students' needs were identified, score and sequence charts were developed and tried out. The need for joint planning became apparent. The process used for elementary grades can be adapted for middle and higher grades.

Avann, Mike and Kath Wood. *User Education in Art and Design: Theory into Practice.* Art Libraries Society, 1980.

This is a comprehensive survey of present theory and practice in user education for art and design students in the United Kingdom. It covers user education in architecture, fashion design, fine arts, graphic design, art history, textile design and three-dimensional design. Bibliographies are included.

Callard, Joanne C. "The Medical Librarian's Role as Adjunct Faculty Member of a College Within a Health Sciences Center." *Bulletin of the Medical Library Association* 67 (October, 1979): 399–400.

Discussion of the role of librarians as liaison to specific departments or schools based on experiences at the University of Oklahoma Health Sciences Center Library and the College of Pharmacy. Two major responsibilities of the liaison are collection development and library instruction.

Mirsky, Roy M. and John E. Christensen. "Computer-Assisted Legal Research Instruction in Texas Law School." *Law Library Journal* 73 (Winter, 1980): 79–98.

Texas law schools are beginning to address the need for acquainting law students with computer-assisted legal research systems by emphasizing the importance of providing quality instruction for the use of these systems by surveying various approaches to such instruction and by discussing the administrative and instructional challenges posed by data base searching. Appended is information on how LEXIS works and exercises to teach the use of it.

Port, Jane S. "Continuing Education in Information Retrieval Techniques for Clinicians." *Bulletin of the Medical Library Association* 68 (1980): 238–240.

At Mount Sinai Medical Center user education is offered to nurses, medical students and other users for continuing education units in a two-hour program.

Risoli, Toni and others. "Instruction in Data Base Searching at the State Library." *Bookmark* 38 (Fall, 1979): 261–263.

Discusses the training for data base searches involving some publicity and dispelling of user hesitation.

Sewell, Winifred and others. "Integrating Library Skills Teaching into the Pharmacy School Curriculum." *American Journal of Pharmaceutical Education* 44 (February, 1980): 65--70.

A subcommittee of the University of Maryland School of Pharmacy Curriculum Committee recommended 11 basic library skills for undergraduate students to be incorporated into the school of pharmacy curriculum. The committee stated the goals in terms of student competencies in the use of published literature to obtain information as an effective alternative to other means of solving problems. Various courses which incorporate the teaching of these skills are described and evaluation is discussed.

ALL LEVELS

Brenner, Lisa and others. "User-Computer Interface Designs for Information Systems: A Review." *Library Research* 2 (Spring, 1980--81): 63--73.

Discusses the need for librarians to develop methodology to help information seekers utilize computer systems. It will be necessary to provide information retrieval systems which require no special knowledge to use for end users. Research relevant to improved user access to online systems is reviewed.

Davinson, Donald. "Instruction in Library User." In *Reference Service*. London: Bingley, 1980, pp. 175--205.

Elias, Arthur W. and others. "End User Education: A Design Study." *Online Review* 4 (June, 1980): 153--162.

Describes a workshop sponsored by BIOSIS and with the Ibum Associates communications consultants to develop educational programs for end users of a data base. End users include educators, students and managers.

Kenney, Donald J. "Universal Library Skills: An Outdated Concept." *The Southeastern Librarian* 30 (Spring, 1980): 13--14.

Discusses how librarians in different libraries view library skills training for users quite differently. Advocates teaching universal library skills by beginning to mold users' attitudes and values toward the library and by helping them to develop reasoning skills. This will help prepare for the future and the changing technology.

Lubans, John, Jr. "Library Literacy." *RQ* 19 (Summer, 1980): 325--328.

The author discusses the lack of meaningful administrative

support for library instruction especially in a large research library and the difficulty of evaluating library instruction. Sound suggestions for evaluation techniques are provided based on examples of formative and summative evaluation from the CRL--NEH program at the University of Colorado.

Morse, Grant W. *Guide to the Incomparable New York Times Index.* New York: Fleet Academic Editions, Inc., 1980.

Provides a detailed guide on the use of the *New York Times Index* and suggests application to many research activities. Gives information on the history and development of this index.

On-Site Library Training Program for School and Community in an Economically and Culturally Deprived County. ERIC Document Reproduction Service, 1979. ED 183 136.

The planning and procedures for a year-long comprehensive in-service library training program for students, teachers, administrators, college, public and school librarians in the rural area of Holmes County in Mississippi are described. Evaluation procedures, publicity, promotion ideas, etc. are appended.

Rader, Hannelore B. "Reference Services as a Teaching Function." *Library Trends* 29 (Summer, 1980): 95--103.

Discusses how instructing the library user is part of the reference function in libraries by teaching the user on a one-to-one basis and providing guides.

Radford, Neil A. "Why Bother with Reader Education?" *New Zealand Libraries* 43 (December, 1980): 53--56.

Examines the need for library user education. Criticizes library instruction literature for its low quality. Discusses reasons for so many user education programs. Gives some alternatives to user education programs. Expresses doubt in the value of reader education unless it is executed extremely well.

Renford, Beverly and Linnea Hendrickson. *Bibliographic Instruction: A Handbook.* New York: Neal-Schuman Publishers, Inc., 1980.

The purpose of this handbook is to serve as a practical guide for librarians involved in developing or improving library-user education programs and activities. A variety of areas within bibliographic instruction are covered such as planning, orientation, guides, course-related instruction, workbooks, credit courses, computer-assisted instruction and audio visual materials. The book includes examples, practical applications and many references.

Sharma, Ravindra N. "Bibliographic Education: An Overview." *Libri* 29 (December, 1979): 329--341.

Author gives brief historical development of bibliographic instruction to the present. Also includes discussion of methods, problems and some solutions.

Strawn, Richard R. *Topics, Terms, and Research Techniques: Self-Instruction in Using Library Catalogs.* Metuchen, NJ: Scarecrow Press, Inc., 1980.

This self-instruction workbook is aimed at high school and college students, library aides and technicians to teach them how to read Library of Congress catalog cards, how to use subject headings and subdivisions, how to go from general concepts to specific ones and vice versa, how to apply everyday terms to subject heading terms and how the filing system in the card catalog operates. The manual utilizes pre-tests, exercises and summaries. Answers to the exercises are supplied. The author estimates that it may take from 4 to 7 hours to complete the workbook.

ELEVENTH ANNUAL LIBRARY INSTRUCTION CONFERENCE

May 7 & 8, 1981

EASTERN MICHIGAN UNIVERSITY

REGISTRANTS

Leland G. Alkire, Jr.
Reference and Periodicals Librarian
Eastern Washington University
Cheney, WA 99004

Olivia Andrea
Academic Consultant
Kenosha Unified Schools
Kenosha, WI 53140

Vicki Anders
Bibliographic Instr. Librarian
Texas A&M University
College Station, TX 77843

Dr. Thomas V. Atkins
Deputy Chairman
Baruch College
17 Lexington Ave.
New York, NY 10010

Judith Avery
Instruction Librarian
University of Michigan
Ann Arbor, MI 48109

Rosa B. Babcock
Resource Consultant
El Centro College
Dallas, TX 75202

Betsy Baker
Assistant Ref. Librarian

University of Illinois
Urbana, IL 61801

James A. Belz
Ref. Lib./Coord. of B.I.
University of Wisconsin
Milwaukee, WI 53211

Ann Bevilacqua
Reference Librarian
Franklin & Marshall College
Lancaster, PA 17604

Mary Biggs
Ed. Asst. – Library Quarterly
University of Chicago
Chicago, IL 60637

Brenda Blackburn
Orientation Librarian
IUPUI
Indianapolis, IN 46202

Ann Breitenwischer
Information Services Lib.
Ferris State College
Big Rapids, MI 49307

Barbara Brock
Librarian/Instructor
University of Toledo
Toledo, OH 43606

Denise Brown
Ref./Orientation Librarian
Johnson C. Smith University
Charlotte, NC 28216

Juanita W. Buddy
Curriculum Specialist
Akron Public Schools
Akron, OH 44301

Carol F. Burroughs
Head of Public Services
Gonzaga University
Spokane, WA 99238

Eileen Carpino
Library Director
Wheeling College
Wheeling, WV 26003

Mary Agnes Chase
Reference Librarian
College of St. Catherine
St. Paul, MN 55105

Martin Courtois
Assistant Reference Librarian
University of Illinois
Chicago, IL 60680

Eileen Dubin
Assoc. Head of Circulation
Northern Illinois University
DeKalb, IL 60115

Sherry S. DuPree
Assistant Reference Librarian
University of Florida
Gainesville, FL 32611

Justin DuVall
Assistant Librarian
St. Meinrad College
St. Meinrad, IN 47577

Phyllis Eisenberg
Reference Librarian
Piedmont Virginia Com-
    munity College
Charlottesville, VA 22901

Elizabeth A. Elkins
Assoc. Lib./Acting Director
SUNY — College of Environ.
    Sci. & Forestry
Syracuse, NY 13210

Laine Farley
Humanities Librarian
Stephen F. Austin State
    University
Nacogdoches, TX 75962

Deborah Fink
Reference/Instruction Lib.
University of Colorado
Boulder, CO 80309

Gloria R. Freimer
Education Specialist
University of Toledo
Toledo, OH 43615

Sr. Mary Joan Gleason
Faculty Services Librarian
Nazareth College of
    Rochester
Rochester, NY 14610

Lyle E. Grooters
Media Services Coord./Lib.
St. Clair Community College
Port Huron, MI 48060

Betty L. Hacker
Assistant Ref. Librarian
Colorado State University
Fort Collins, CO 80523

Stella F. Mosborg
Assistant Reference Librarian
University of Illinois
Urbana, IL 61801

Constance P. Mulligan
Instr. Services Coordinator
Northern Kentucky University
Highland Heights, KY 41076

Gail Oltmanns
Ref./Instruction Librarian
Indiana University
Bloomington, IN 47405

Joyce Payne
Reference Librarian
Hofstra University
Hempstead, NY 11010

Carol B. Penka
Reference Librarian
University of Illinois
Urbana, IL 61801

Oswell Person
Dean Learning Resource Services
Mission College
Santa Clara, CA 95054

Billie Peterson
Reference Librarian
Ohio State University
Columbus, OH 43210

Linda J. Piele
Head, Public Services Division
University of Wisconsin
Kenosha, WI 53141

Audrey K. Potter
Reference Librarian
Simmons College
Boston, MA 02115

Ms. Virginia L. Powell
Lib. of Music, Ed. & Audio
    Visual
Wheaton College
Wheaton, IL 60187

Hannelore B. Rader
Director
University of Wisconsin
Kenosha, WI 53141

Fred R. Reenstjerna
Librarian — Hollins Branch
Roanoke County Pub. Lib.
Roanoke, VA 24019

Marty Reimers
Ref. & Media Service Lib.
Butler County Community
    College
Butler, PA 16001

Glenn Remelts
Public Service Librarian
Beloit College
Beloit, WI 53511

Jean Rexer
Media Specialist
Trenton High School
Trenton, MI 48183

Rosemary Rice-Billings
Reference Librarian
Saginaw Valley State College
University Center, MI 48710

Linda S. Richer
Associate Librarian
Goshen College
Goshen, IN 46526

Thomas Risto
Director Learning Resource
    Center

Wayne County Community
College
Redford, MI 48239

Anne Roberts
Associate Librarian
SUNY Library
Albany, NY 12222

Craig Robertson
Reference Librarian
University of Wisconsin--
Parkside
Kenosha, WI 53141

Ina N. Robertson
Instr. Services Librarian
Sangamon State University
Springfield, IL 62708

Diane Ruess
Assistant Librarian
SUNY — College of Environ.
Sci. & Forestry
Syracuse, NY 13210

Christine Ryan
Reference Librarian
Dartmouth College
Hanover, NH 03755

Carol Lee Saffioti
Faculty-Assistant Professor
University of Wisconsin--
Parkside
Kenosha, WI 53141

Lou Helen Sanders
Instruction of Library Science
Jackson State University
Jackson, MS 39219

Patricia Renn-Scanlan
Reference Librarian
DePauw University
Greencastle, IN 46135

Mary Grace Sell
Coord., Ref. & Public Service
Westmoreland County Com-
munity College
Youngwood, PA 15697

Rose Marie Service
Education-Psychology Lib.
University of Oregon
Eugene, OR 97403

Tom Sharrard
Director: Lib./Media Services
Wayne-Westland Community
Schools
Wayne, MI 48184

Karen Sherrard
Librarian
Olivet College
Olivet, MI 49224

Sheila Smith
Learning Res. Center Coord.
Wayne County Community
College
Detroit, MI 48226

Ruth Stephenson
Associate Director
Spring Arbor College
Spring Arbor, MI 49283

Renee F. Stiff
Orientation/Instr. Librarian
Johnson C. Smith University
Charlotte, NC 28216

Carla Stoffle
Assistant Chancellor
University of Wisconsin--
Parkside
Kenosha, WI 53141

John C. Tyson
Asst. to Director of Libraries
Northern Illinois University
Dekalb, IL 60115

Michael VanHouten
Reference Librarian
Albion College
Albion, MI 49224

James E. Ward
Director of the Library
David Lipscomb College
Nashville, TN 37203

Paula Warnken
Coord. of Reader Services
Xavier University
Cincinnati, OH 45207

Rayda Warren
Media Specialist
John Glenn High School
Wayne, MI 48185

Elizabeth Wavle
Public Services Librarian
Elmira College
Elmira, NY 14901

Cynthia M. Whitacre
Reference Librarian
DePauw University
Greencastle, IN 46135

Calvin Williams
Head - Reference Services
Saginaw Valley State College
University Center, MI 48710

Brian Yamel
Reference Librarian
University of Wisconsin–
    Parkside
Kenosha, WI 53141

Sandra Yee
Coord. for Library Services
Muskegon Community
    College
Muskegon, MI 49441